ALBERT MEHRABIAN, Ph.D.

YOUR

INNER

PATH TO

INVESTMENT

SUCCESS

Insights into the Psychology of Investing

FOREWORD BY CARTER RANDALL

PROBUS PUBLISHING COMPANY
Chicago, Illinois

Library of Congress Cataloging in Publication Data Available

ISBN 1-55738-210-7

Printed in the United States of America

BB

1   2   3   4   5   6   7   8   9   0

Table of Contents

Foreword

So much has been written and said about how to choose investments—so-called new, innovative methods of making money, strategies for analyzing the economy and social trends and, therefore, investing to adapt to all of these things.

Now, finally, we have available a book on one of the most important subjects of them all, the way in which investors take stock of themselves, recognize their weaknesses and strengths, take advantage of them or, conversely, suppress them.

Often overlooked is the subjective side of investing. More important than the objective, it deals with the needs, goals, psyches, and circumstances of individual investors. And it is vital that investors understand themselves, what they are trying to accomplish, how they may react to success or failure, and finally, doing whatever is necessary to achieve in their own minds satisfaction with the management of their money.

Such satisfaction is not necessarily produced by achieving great wealth. In fact, for many great wealth often breeds anxiety coupled with a feeling of responsibility to do even better, and often investors become slaves to their money rather than masters of it.

I have known many successful investors, some who have been publicly recognized as such but others who have not. They all have several things in common even though their methodology has been different.

First, they all take a long view. That is, they are untroubled by short-term events and look ahead to what they observe are (correctly of course) long-term trends in the economic, social and political areas.

Second, they are flexible, able to adjust to changing times and conditions.

Third, they have pre-determined disciplines enabling them to know ahead of time what they will do, given opportunities.

Fourth, they continuously strive to improve their knowledge and understanding of various investment markets and individual investments.

Fifth, they seek advice from others whom they consider knowledgeable, not necessarily following all the advice they get but at least absorbing it.

Sixth, they are humble, not doubting their ability but recognizing and admitting that they do make mistakes.

Seventh, they have enough confidence in themselves to take action on their investments in accordance with what they think.

Eighth, they are intelligent.

Ninth, (the most important of all) they work hard.

On the pages that follow, Albert Mehrabian examines in depth how specific psyches affect investors and what individual investors should consider and do as a result of self analysis. It behooves individual investors to pay attention, and as a matter of fact, professional advisors should also tune in because they too are emotional beings, and they too should adjust to the psyches of their clients. This is the basis of successful investing is all about.

B. Carter Randall
Panelist
Wall Street Week
 with Louis Rukeyser

Chapter 1

Introduction

Investment success or failure is a function of (a) expertise in the technical and fundamental aspects of investing, and (b) the investor's psychological makeup and awareness. As much as 95 percent of the current investment literature deals with technical and fundamental issues. These are the supply and demand forces acting upon any investment vehicle, economic factors, fundamental values (e.g., balance sheet, earning potential), or price and volume fluctuations. Ability to understand the many factors that govern price movements is, of course, necessary for investment success. When investors have no such preparation, it is important that they recognize the deficiency and turn to more competent sources for guidance or for outright management of their funds.

But, adequate knowledge of technical and fundamental aspects of investing hardly guarantees success. Many highly qualified persons work diligently at investing year after year, learning more as they go along, and still fail to produce returns commensurate with their knowledge and efforts. Oftentimes, massive financial resources and heavy investments of time and effort produce returns comparable to those achieved in comfort and without expertise from savings accounts. Worse still, high levels of effort sometimes produce frequent small gains that are wiped out by occasional large losses.

Yet, there are those who may be less knowledgeable, but who are able to concentrate on some small part of an investment field and develop a reasonably straight-forward strategy that works well. Such individuals some-times begin with meager sums and, through repeated and patient application of the same investment pattern, man-age to amass great wealth to the utter amazement of their relatives and friends.

The intangible factors which sometimes permit the amateur to achieve great success or at times hinder the investment performance of the seasoned professional are psychological ones. Unfortunately, these psychological forces take on a multitude of guises, depending on a particular investment vehicle and specific circumstances associated with it. The greater the complexity of an in-vestment, the easier it is for contributions of psycholog-ical factors to be camouflaged and remain unrecognized. Difficulties and poor performance are then blamed on lack of technical knowledge, absence of reliable informa-tion, or bad luck.

I have watched many of my friends and acquaint-ances go about making investments, pulled about in one or another direction by psychological forces, while being completely oblivious to those effects. On occasion, re-flex-like and psychologically determined actions are ben-eficial to their investments. But, more often than not, these inner forces interfere with wise investment choices or deter continued implementation of sound investment strategies.

Investments involve the making and losing of money and thus arouse the strongest of emotions. The power of investments to affect us with such force is especially noteworthy because investing usually is not a passing or short-lived activity. Once we commit to an investment, it becomes a significant part of our lives. At times, it even resembles an intimate companion—it can please us and make us happy, it can bore, disappoint, bewilder, enthrall, excite, or enrage, and it can induce distress, anxiety, or greed, and even terrify. We can experience some of these emotions even from a single investment we buy and hold.

The ability of investments to arouse strong and varied emotions brings out many personal, deep-seated, and idiosyncratic characteristics of an investor. Like intimate companions, investments elicit some of our most elemental and raw, uncensored, or unguarded inclinations. And, these basic characteristics that come into play in our most intimate relationships or in our handling of investments can be understood in terms of emotional predispositions—our temperaments.

"Temperament" was a concept used in medieval physiology to describe the distinctive physical and psychological qualities of a person. Specifically, the psychological characteristics that distinguished people from one another were analyzed in terms of emotional makeup or emotional predispositions. These emotional predispositions were viewed as being determined by proportions of the four "humors" (blood, phlegm, black and yellow bile) in a person. Preponderance of one or another humor led to four temperament types. Excess of yellow bile resulted in an emotional predisposition to anger (the choleric temperament), preponderance of black bile led to an emotional inclination toward boredom (melancholic temperament), excess of phlegm resulted in an emotional predisposition to relaxation and calm (phlegmatic temperament), and predominance of blood was associated with the emotional characteristic of exuberance (sanguine temperament).

Our current knowledge of physiology, of course, disqualifies "humors" as a basis of temperament. Nevertheless, the idea of emotional predispositions as basic to understanding how people differ psychologically from one another is sound. *Each of us tends to have well-defined emotional habits or characteristics that permeate our approaches to our social relationships, work, play, or investments.* These emotional characteristics become more apparent in certain circumstances, as when we are under pressure or stress or when we find ourselves in highly emotional situations.

Investments, insofar as they are a source of strong emotions, activate these deep-seated, unconscious, or reflex-like habits and actions associated with temperament. Two people can be equally knowledgeable in the stock market, but one of them may have a tremendous record of success while the other experiences repeated failures.

To understand such differences in investment success and failure that are not determined by differences in technical knowledge, we must examine the role of temperament. Some emotional characteristics make it easy for one to succeed, other characteristics get in the way of success.

The important thing about these emotional characteristics is that they typically lead to identifiable and repetitious investment patterns for each person. One investor may buy with the intention to hold until his investment doubles, but sell as soon as he has a ten percent profit. Another one may invest only when there is a strong popular consensus that the investment will lead to profit. A third investor may be unnecessarily active, trading frequently, even though a much slower pace of transactions could be more profitable and entail lower trading costs.

As we shall see, *the investment patterns favored by each individual are simply another manifestation of his or her emotional characteristics or temperament.* Some investors are introspective enough to recognize the regularities in their investment tactics and thus can identify these patterns. Others fail to recognize the patterns because superficial differences in their various investments seemingly involve considerably diverse reasons for purchases and sales and the underlying form or pattern of action remains undetected.

Whether investors recognize these patterns or not, most fail to see the associations the patterns have with their own temperaments. This is because they do not have the psychological and analytical tools to understand their own actions and compare and contrast these with investment patterns of others who have different temperaments.

This volume is designed to provide readers with the basic tools to identify their temperaments and the investment patterns typically associated with those temperaments. Readers can discover investment strengths and weaknesses brought on by their emotional characteristics, they can learn about investment forms most suited to their particular combinations of strengths and weaknesses, and they can become aware of safeguards they need to prevent losses caused by emotional reactions to investments.

Aside from temperament, and to analyze the match or mismatch between temperament and investment, we also must consider the differing emotional effects of various investments. The world of investments includes a wide array of instruments or vehicles, each of which is capable of arousing distinctive ranges or qualities of emotion. Emotions aroused by savings accounts versus those associated with active trading in highly leveraged commodities or financial futures are worlds apart—the first involves monotony, boredom, or comfort, whereas the second can result in bewilderment, excitement, or terror.

Successful investing requires a proper match between investor temperament and investment type. Some temperament qualities allow investors to deal successfully with highly emotional investments; other qualities lead them to make repeated, similar, and costly errors when attempting to deal with such investments.

This volume provides a framework to categorize investments in terms of their emotional effects. It provides a descriptive system to describe all types of temperament. It also contains an analysis of successful and unsuccessful combinations of investments and temperaments.

Specifically, concepts from information theory are used in Chapter 3 to characterize the "uncertainty" (complexity, variation, rate of change, and novelty) of different investments. "Uncertainty" is essential for understanding differences in emotional reactions to various investments. Chapters 4 through 6 contain descriptions of investment-related strengths and weaknesses associated with each of three basic, and research-based, dimensions of temperament. Combinations of these three basic dimensions yield eight derivative temperament types that are sketched first in Chapter 7 and then considered individually in each of eight subsequent chapters.

The various chapters on temperament contain descriptions of social-, work-, and investment-related characteristics and choices associated with each temperament. They also contain analyses of successes or failures in investor-investment matches and ways to achieve better matches, thereby safeguarding against psychologically determined errors in investing.

In addition to temperament, one's life circumstances also have important bearing on investment actions. Someone who has a generally peaceful and comfortable work and family situation is prone to approach her investments differently than one who is continually burdened with conflicts and problems at work or at home. A person who suddenly comes into a lot of money will handle investments differently from one who has gradually accumulated the same amount over the course of many years.

The advantage of the present framework for analysis of temperament is that it can be translated and applied readily to understand the effects of life circumstances. This is the subject of Chapter 16 which deals with the emotional impact of varying life circumstances and ways in which this impact affects investment behaviors for better or worse.

This volume provides readers with insights into temperament—a psychological characteristic that is at the core of personality, interpersonal relationships, and psychological problems. Since our description of people is comprehensive, it covers both good and bad qualities of temperament, thus shedding a negative, and possibly discouraging, light on half the temperament types described. Readers who detect some of these undesirable characteristics in themselves should not give up in despair. Awareness of handicaps, together with the guidelines provided, should help readers redirect their efforts so as to compensate for temperament-related handicaps. Chapter 18, in particular, contains an overview of how one can adjust one's investment choices to compensate for deficiencies caused by temperament and/or life circumstances. A general formula is provided and can be used to calculate the level of investment uncertainty suited to any combination of temperament and life situation.

Chapter 2
Cases

Roger has a very large law practice and employs approximately twenty persons. Despite the size of his practice
and many opportunities to generate a respectable income
from it, he usually is in debt and struggling to meet his
payroll. Many of his financial difficulties emanate from
unwise investments rather than from the way in which
he conducts his business.

Roger is almost addicted to new investment ideas
that might generate unusually large profits. Just about
anyone with a wild and convoluted investment scheme
can call him, and despite Roger's busy schedule, gain
access to him to discuss the investment.

These promoters usually walk away with a five- or
ten- thousand-dollar check as initial payment on an investment which serious consideration would reveal to be
worthless. Their secret, however, is they do not approach
Roger with dull proposals to make him somewhere
around 12 percent per year on his capital; instead, they
are likely to suggest a doubling or tripling of his money
within a few months. The wilder, more unrealistic, and
more complicated an investment sounds, the more it
appeals to Roger.

There are confidence artists in the investment world
who prey on the likes of Roger, and word seems to have
gotten around to this group—Roger is on their lists.

Roger is intelligent and is competent in his profession. Somehow, though, when it comes to investing, he loses control, cannot think critically and logically, acts impulsively, and parts with funds which are needed to conduct his business in a normal way. The money drain affects the rest of Roger's work. Frequent employee layoffs in efforts to economize have an adverse effect on morale, and it is increasingly difficult for him to hire and retain high-caliber employees.

What psychological force is at the core of Roger's problem? The simple answer is a tendency toward boredom, not caused by life circumstances but rather by temperament. "Temperament" refers to a person's emotional characteristics which are relatively stable over a lifetime. Some people are generally happy and pleasant—more so than most others. This does not mean they do not experience unhappiness, frustration, or anger. Rather, it means the temperamentally happy individual, on the average and across all kinds of situations, is generally happier than most. Roger's temperament or emotional makeup is biased toward boredom: in comparison with others, he is more likely to feel depressed, unhappy, tired, unenthusiastic, sleepy, or helplessly trapped. As a consequence, he is likely to find his work routines or his home life unstimulating, monotonous, tiresome, or worse, hopeless and depressing.

There are a great variety of constructive, or harmful, ways to counteract boredom. To understand how Roger goes about it, we need to know that excitement is the perfect antidote to boredom. Some people use drugs such as amphetamines, cocaine, or other stimulants to generate a temporary high and gain brief relief from boredom. Others constructively engage in sports where the opportunity to meet and interact with different persons and the emotional arousal from physical activity combine to create feelings like excitement.

For Roger, excitement is provided by fantasies relating to his investments and the variety of skillful, manipulative, and up-beat characters who approach him with investment ideas. Obviously, an investment which provides a reasonably safe return of 15 percent year after year could not generate sufficient excitement to allay Roger's boredom. Instead, he needs something unusual, complicated, and challenging—something that has the earmarks of a great investment breakthrough, involves complicated wheeling and dealing, legal maneuvering, and the promise of very large profits. This is the kind of fertile material for endless weeks of fantasy, something to keep his mind busy and on a hopeful, up-beat note until he is forcefully and inexorably convinced it is a lost cause.

The use of unrealistic and loss-prone investments as an escape from boredom is a common syndrome, but the problem usually escapes detection unless investors seek psychological help from a professional. Usually, the victim and his friends and relatives think the losses are due to lack of expertise, a tendency to take bad risks, naivete, or gullibility.

Unfortunately, Roger is not aware of how his boredom contributes to his investment style and failures. He is aware only of the driven and pressured way in which he approaches each investment, the subsequent failure, the resolution to be more careful next time, and, soon thereafter, yet another desperate effort. Within himself, Roger admits to having some kind of addiction, but this admission is not useful because it implies the problem is beyond his control. If, on the other hand, Roger were to become aware of the emotional base of his behavior, he would discover alternative ways to alleviate the boredom without having to suffer massive financial losses. It is our task here to help people like Roger become aware of the emotional bases of their investment tactics and to direct them toward fruitful investments compatible with their emotional makeup.

The problem does not have to be as serious as boredom to result in large and unaffordable losses from investments. Jim who was single and lived alone, worked out of his house and tended to be socially isolated. Although he had dates about twice a week, this did not provide him with sufficient social stimulation. What he needed was a mate at home to develop a richer and more active social life.

Jim invested in the stock market and traded actively through three different brokers. He had developed excellent rapport with one of these brokers, Murray, who was friendly and knowledgeable. They often called each other after the market closed and talked for about half an hour to analyze the day's events, hot stocks to trade, and to plan buying and selling strategies.

Jim progressively concentrated his trades in the account with Murray. Their working relationship was strengthened during an up-trend in the stock market when they usually executed trades daily and did so with reasonable success. During this period, they developed a bond of mutual respect for each other's stock market know-how and instinctive sense for timely trades. So, when occasionally Murray suggested something rather risky, Jim tended to go along, partly because he felt like pleasing this new-found friend.

This cozy arrangement began to fall apart during a five-week market decline. As prices moved steadily downward, Jim found himself invested heavily in a variety of high-risk stock option calls which rapidly declined in value—far more rapidly than the declines in the corresponding stocks.

Jim and Murray still had their usual chats and analyzed the market. They agreed that the decline was temporary, offered other explanations as to why the original purchase decisions were indeed correct, and felt they would pull things off by waiting patiently. But, alas, the waiting led to additional paper losses and eventually to complete loss of Jim's invested capital, including large sums he had borrowed to invest.

Unlike Roger's, Jim's problem was not so much a function of the kind of person he was or his temperament, but more so a result of his life circumstances at the time he got involved heavily in the stock market. Lengthy periods of living and working alone had created a strong need in him for a good friend or companion— someone he could respect and trust and with whom he could share some of the more intense events in his life. This someone turned out to be a broker and led to feelings of mutual respect and false confidence which resulted in a massive financial disaster for Jim.

Had Jim been aware of the psychological underpinning of his relationship with Murray, he would have been more skeptical of his moderate successes in the rising market. It is easy to make money in the stock market during a bull move; indeed, he could have made more had he not traded as frequently. Also, awareness of his need might have led him to seek adequate companionship in his daily life and would have lessened the importance and frequency of contacts with Murray. In that case, Jim probably would have approached other experts for advice during the market downturn because he wouldn't have felt as confident. More than likely, he would have been advised to sell his options quickly, conserve his cash, and wait for another opportunity to get back in the market.

Our discussions in this volume frequently deal with investment problems to illustrate underlying psychological processes that interfere with success. Examples of persons who invest successfully also are used to analyze the complementary psychological qualities associated with investment achievements.

Douglas is one such example of the low-key and highly successful investor. He is a sociology professor with a moderate salary but manages to save about $2,500 per year.

Douglas began to get involved in the stock market through his readings and developed a particular style of investing very much in tune with his temperament. In the seventies, his stock broker had mentioned a certain company that, among many others, somehow peaked Douglas' interest. This company had considerable hidden assets and its stock was selling at a large discount relative to its net asset value. This interested Douglas because it had the earmarks of safety. He requested charts of price movements of the stock over time and studied the charts and followed the daily price quotes for several months without investing any money in the market.

Following several months of careful deliberation, Douglas had a growing conviction he had a feeling for the history of price changes in this particular issue. The stock price had fluctuated between $7 and $13 for several years. Douglas decided that the stock was a reasonably safe purchase at about $7 per share. He waited patiently for several more months and the opportunity did indeed present itself. The stock market had taken a large drop, most share prices were depressed and Douglas was able to use his $10,000 savings to buy 2,500 shares of the company's stock on "margin." This means he borrowed an additional $8,000 from his stockbroker to make the purchase.

Having successfully identified the low end of price fluctuations and having acted upon this, Douglas was confident at this point. Following his strategy, he waited for the stock price to move toward the high end of the $7 to $13 range. He focused primarily on this particular issue, continued studying its price charts, noted its daily price and volume changes, and ignored the many temptations and fears generated by stock market commentators, advisers, and news reports. Within a year and a half, the stock price slowly and erratically moved up so that for a period of two or three weeks it traded between $12 and $13 per share. Douglas sold his entire position at this juncture, selling a few hundred shares at a time, and averaging around $12.50 per share. After interest payments to the broker and repayment of the $8,000 loan, he was left with about $22,000 cash in his account.

By now Douglas had developed his own distinctive investment style. He asked his broker to inform him about other similar undervalued stocks. In the meantime, he continued to monitor the stock he had just sold. To him, it seemed like a familiar and old friend. Within a year, the stock market had taken another drop and his favorite stock was once again trading below $8. Douglas bought 3,000 shares this time around.

During the waiting period, Douglas had learned about a second company in a different line of business which he had followed studiously. This, too, was a small company listed on the New York Exchange that had never traded under $3 per share during the previous 20 years. The ongoing bear market had hammered down the price of this particular issue to $3.50. Feeling that he was safely close to the lowest price of the stock for many years, Douglas purchased 3,000 shares of this issue as well. This time Douglas borrowed about $12,000 from his broker to make the two sets of purchases.

Within two years, he sold the stock of the first company at above $12 per share. Since his original stock served as a yardstick of market ups and downs, it helped him decide to sell the stock of the second company during the same period, obtaining around $7 per share for the latter. After sale of both stocks and repayment of the loan and interest, Douglas now had $45,000 in his account.

Simple and outlandish as it may sound, after waiting patiently, Douglas had another opportunity to purchase the stock of the first company near the $7 mark. By now, this stock served as his gauge for general market conditions—when it approached $7, the stock market was cheap and it was time to buy, when it approached $13, the stock market was expensive and it was time to sell.

Douglas never owned more than three stocks at any one time and the two mentioned were part of his portfolio in 1981. By then, he had moved into bigger leagues. His trading vehicle was IBM stock which he felt was undervalued at around $50 per share and of which he owned 1,600 shares. His style had not changed since his early days of investing. He waited patiently, buying when the stock he studied for many long months looked inexpensive and waited patiently again to sell when it started looking expensive. In the meantime, whether he owned them or not at any given time, every day he followed the price movements of the very few stocks which interested him.

The investment style Douglas developed was distinctive and natural for him. It fitted perfectly his temperament of being careful, painstaking in planning, extremely patient, able to delay gratification, and most importantly, independent-minded and confident in his methodical approach. As we shall see, Douglas has a "relaxed" temperament. Not everyone with this temperament can be a successful investor. But generally, a methodical, patient, and realistically-based investment approach is likely to bear beneficial results for relaxed persons.

Quite a different investment style is exemplified by Jennifer who always seems to be in the hottest and most talked-about investment of the day. She loves to discuss her investments, whether these are real estate one year, gold and silver another, and stocks the next. She willingly reveals details of her investment activities to co-workers and friends, talks with an authoritative air, and tends to emphasize her more successful exploits. Jennifer does not invest large amounts which she could not afford to lose; she dabbles using small sums and loves every minute of it.

Jennifer has an "exuberant" temperament. She is outgoing, likes to take charge of situations, and is pleasant. She enjoys socializing and her investments provide a vehicle for interesting social exchanges. Over the years, her friends have learned that they can turn to Jennifer for preliminary advice if they need information about various investments.

Jennifer generally loses some money on her investments each year. But, the losses are not painful and are compensated for by the excitement and novelty of her investment-related experiences and by the fun she has showing off. For her, investments are a casual hobby which cost some money each year.

Donald presents a sharp contrast to Jennifer. He exemplifies the investor with strong convictions about a certain class of investments and combines this with patience, determination, and flexibility. His love is real estate. In the early sixties, while still a graduate student at UCLA, he purchased his first family home in a distant suburb for $14,000. His downpayment was $500. Six months later, due to some appreciation of prices in his neighborhood, he was able to refinance his home and borrow more money against it. He used the $2,000 cash proceeds from refinancing as downpayment on another, larger house. He rented the second house and since rental income did not quite cover expenses, his wife took on a part-time job to make up the deficit.

Fortunately for Donald, this initial period was one of rising real estate values. He soon sold the first home he had purchased, paid off the bank and used the profit as downpayment on a four-unit apartment building. Once again, about a year after purchasing that building, he was able to refinance and extract cash from the investment. He continued to pyramid in this way until about 1970 when he owned several single-family homes and a couple of apartment buildings scattered throughout Los Angeles.

Donald had a strong belief in the ultimate worth of real estate. His strategy was to shop carefully, buy cheaply in a rising market, and then refinance to obtain cash for additional purchases. When the "negative" (expenses minus income) became burdensome, he sold one of his properties and used the proceeds to make up the negative cash flow.

Real estate values declined in 1970, and again in 1975, forcing Donald to sell some of his holdings at disadvantageous prices. However, increases in rental income helped during these difficult periods and firm belief in his method encouraged him to persist and stay the course.

Beginning in 1976, with the gradual and accelerating onset of a most virulent inflationary period, Donald's conviction about the soundness of investing in real estate started to pay off in a big way. He formed small partnerships and purchased single-family homes, very large apartment buildings, and office buildings whenever he could drive an advantageous bargain. He was flexible in that he sold when he received a good purchase offer on one of his properties. For instance, during 1979 and 1980, he sold some of his commercial buildings for over one million dollars each and used the proceeds to pay off many smaller loans on properties he had purchased a few years earlier.

Throughout 1981–1984, he comfortably waited out the real estate downturn in California. During this period, he bought heavily discounted properties with an eye to five or seven years hence when he was convinced the real estate market once again would be humming along.

Donald has a calm, unemotional, and introverted temperament referred to as "disdainful." A disdainful temperament resembles the relaxed one in two important ways but differs from it in a third way—relaxed persons are more pleasant than disdainful ones. Donald's temperament has permitted him to follow his investment strategy patiently and methodically without being derailed by contrary advice or persuasion of others. His game plan does not collapse during temporary setbacks because it includes the safety net of sales and relief from excessive debt. Also, he does not deviate from his strategy at such difficult times because his temperament attenuates the effects of stress and its associated anxiety.

Our last case is taken from commodities trading where participants purchase or sell gold, silver, wheat, corn, or oil, for instance, against future delivery. Such trading is usually extremely high-paced and risky because of leverage. Low deposits of about ten percent of the purchase or sale price are used to control (buy or sell) large quantities of a commodity. For example, a buyer may use $6,000 to control $60,000 worth of a commodity. A 10 percent increase in the price of that commodity can double his investment and, conversely, a drop in price can wipe out his capital. Commodities, therefore, are not for the meek. They certainly are not suitable for the anxious or the dependent.

Maxine is an old hand at commodities trading. She has learned the hard way that her buying and selling must be totally unemotional and mechanical. She has written rules about exactly when to initiate a position by buying or selling. She also has rules about what to do when prices move against, or in favor of, her position. Maxine adheres rigidly to these rules despite many temptations to deviate from them. For example, when the price moves against her beyond a fixed percentage of loss, she sells automatically. She leaves absolutely no room for emotions, such as hopes that there might be a change in price trend that will permit her to recover the loss. On the other hand, when the price moves in her favor, she stays put and, at the end of each day, determines a new and higher price level at which she will sell when a reversal occurs.

Even though this kind of mechanical trading sounds easy enough, anyone who has tried the commodities markets knows it takes incredible emotional fortitude to adhere to such rules when large sums are being made and lost in a matter of hours. Maxine has the right kind of determined, calm, and unemotional temperament for this game. Like Douglas, Maxine has a relaxed temperament.

The importance of an unemotional temperament in commodities trading is illustrated by a competition experiment which pegged the top-performing floor trader of a Chicago commodities company against the computer (and rule-based) trading program of a Cupertino, California establishment. Although during the ten-day contest the expert trader achieved an excellent annualized profit of 55 percent on the original amount of investment, the computer program bested this performance with a 120 percent annualized return. Remembering that such a mechanical program is totally devoid of emotional reactions, we see that a low level of emotionality is certainly an asset for investments which involve high risk combined with fast pace and require rapid decision-making.

Chapter 3

Investment Uncertainty

Having your money in a savings bank or in three-month U.S. Treasury bills is different from buying a triple-A rated corporate bond. In the former instances, your capital remains intact plus you earn a specified rate of interest. However, with the corporate bond, even one of high safety rating, there is a small element of risk because market forces determine interest rates. The market value of a corporate bond declines as interest rates rise; it increases as interest rates drop.

The buyer of a corporate bond has greater "uncertainty" than one who deposits funds in savings accounts or with the U.S. Treasury. The bondholder may be forced to sell to meet a financial emergency and he may have to do so at an inopportune time.

The preceding examples represent some of the lowest "uncertainty" investments. How about the lady who makes a $30,000 downpayment on a four-unit apartment building costing $160,000? Let us say the rest of the purchase price is met through a variable interest loan from a bank. Also, assume that income from the units is insufficient to cover the mortgage, taxes, and operating expenses. This investor has a great deal more "uncertainty": property values in her neighborhood may move up or move down, a tenant may fail to make monthly payments, a unit or two may remain vacant too long, the building may require repairs and some repairs may be costly, or a tenant may have a pet dog that is a nuisance to other tenants and a source of headaches to the owner. Also, the owner would have to regularly make up the deficit because the income does not cover all her expenses.

INVESTMENT UNCERTAINTY

We use the concept of "uncertainty" from the mathematical theory of communication to characterize the preceding, and all other, investments. Put simply, the uncertainty level of an investment is high when it is *complex, varied, changing rapidly, unexpected,* and *novel.* Uncertainty of an investment is low when it is *simple, stable, changing slowly, expected,* and *familiar.*

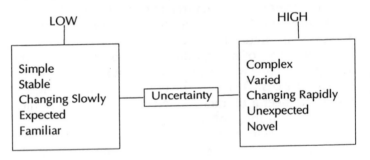

Complexity

"Complexity" refers to the components, events, and actions an investment involves and the interrelationships among all these. When an investor deposits money in a savings account, there are essentially three parts or aspects to the investment: amount invested, interest rate, and date when the money can be withdrawn without penalty.

In comparison, components of an investment in an apartment building are numerous. First, there are the strictly financial aspects including the amount of downpayment, amount owed the bank, interest rate on the loan, loan payments, expenses to operate the building, and taxes. But, these only summarize many additional components, events, and relationships in the act of investing. The owner must see to it that units are rented and rents are collected. She must arrange for regular maintenance of the building and contact and oversee workmen to do repairs when necessary. She must deal with difficult tenants who cannot pay their rents or those who are bothersome to their neighbors. Finally, she must rearrange her personal finances to make up the deficit generated by the investment. According to our definition of "uncertainty," the apartment building, insofar as it is far more complex than a savings account, is a considerably more uncertain investment.

Variation

The "varied vs. stable" quality of an investment is a second important aspect of its uncertainty. Lending money to a savings bank involves no changes during the period of the loan. Once the lending period is over, there may be a change in interest rate, but that is all. The apartment building, on the other hand, involves many changes. Tenants may vacate units, necessitating renewed efforts by the investor to rent those units, income may be delayed or reduced when a tenant is late with the rent or is unable to pay, expenses may increase temporarily due to needed repairs, and workmen who regularly do the maintenance or repairs may become unavailable and new workers would need to be found. Also, remembering that the mortgage is of the variable interest type, the interest rate on the loan may change. Thus, the apartment building is a more uncertain type of investment because its quality is more varied than a savings account.

Rate of Change

"Rate of change" of an investment refers to the speed with which changes occur in the investment. Once again, it is obvious that a savings account involves an exceedingly low rate of change whereas investment in a residential income property can involve more rapid changes. However, the speed at which changes occur in real estate investments is typically much slower than the speed at which changes occur in many other common investments, such as those in stocks, commodities, options, or financial futures. Indeed, with options, commodities, or financial futures, one's investment can change significantly in value even in the course of a single week, and sometimes even in a single day. On the other hand, with real estate investments, changes occur far more slowly, giving the investor a chance to deal with them at a more leisurely (and quite possibly, a more rational) way.

So, although real estate investments tend to involve greater uncertainty because of their more complex and varied qualities, the uncertainty is attenuated considerably because of the slower rates of change.

Unexpected-Expected Quality

"Unexpected vs. expected" changes are yet another important characteristic of investment uncertainty. Savings accounts involve no unexpected changes during the loan period, but involve some change in interest rate when the loan is renewed. In contrast, several of the changes involving the fourplex can be unexpected. Some of the changes are regular, predictable, and planned aspects of the investment program: monthly rents, mortgage payments, taxes, and operating expenses typically tend to be predictable. However, there also can be surprises, as in the case of vacancies, unexpected repair bills, or changes in mortgage interest rates. This, then, is a fourth important way in which investing in the fourplex is more uncertain than lending money to a bank or to the U.S. Treasury.

Novelty-Familiarity

Unlike the preceding four qualities of uncertainty, "novelty vs. familiarity" of an investment is not so much a characteristic of the investment itself, but rather an attribute of the investor. Novelty-familiarity is simply a function of the investor's experience with a particular type of investment. If an investment is a first for the individual, its novelty makes it more uncertain; if, on the other hand, it is very familiar because he has had many similar experiences with the type of investment, then there is no added contribution to uncertainty from this source.

Someone who visits a Federal Reserve Bank for the first time to purchase a U.S. Treasury bill or bond will experience novelty and, therefore, more uncertainty than one who simply deposits funds in a familiar savings account. However, once you have gone through the process of purchasing U.S. Treasury bills or bonds two or three times, the novelty wears off and the uncertainty level approximates that of a savings account.

Similarly, if investing in a building is a first experience of its kind for the owner, then novelty makes a large contribution to uncertainty. If, on the other hand, the investor has owned other buildings and is highly familiar with the workings of such investments, the purchase of yet another building involves little novelty and this aspect does not add to investment uncertainty.

Consideration of novelty permits us to understand in part how the same investment can have differing effects on different persons. The experienced investor has less novelty and less uncertainty and can be more relaxed or calm about the investment, whereas the inexperienced one is more likely to worry and become upset or anxious about the identical project.

Ways to Control Uncertainty

In considering any investment, then, it is important to review all five aspects of its uncertainty: *complexity, variability, rate of change, unexpected quality, and novelty.* Irrespective of what kind of investment medium you select, such as the stock market, you always have a wide range of options on choices of uncertainty. If you desire very low uncertainty, you might select a very conservatively managed fund and purchase its shares. In this case, since you will not be involved directly in the selection, purchase, and sale of various issues, all five aspects of uncertainty will be at low levels. The main changes will consist of changes in your share values and these changes will typically be slow for a conservative fund. On rare occasions, you might sell your shares in the fund and move into cash or into a bond fund, and these decisions temporarily will increase your uncertainty level.

In contrast, someone else might trade the stock market actively, making his own trading decisions. Activity and change could be at a very high pace if stocks were purchased and sold on a weekly basis. There would thus be considerable complexity, rapid change, unexpected events and price moves, and novelty, yielding a very high level of uncertainty for the investor.

Thus, although some investment media are typically high or low in uncertainty — for example, commodities and financial futures tend to be high-uncertainty vehicles whereas bonds or preferred stock issues are low-uncertainty — there are ways in which you can approach each investment medium so as to increase or decrease its uncertainty.

If you maintain your distance from the investment by using investment managers as intermediaries, you, of course, will reduce uncertainty considerably. If you elect a very slow trading pace, this too will reduce uncertainty; in contrast, a high trading pace will increase uncertainty. Staying with highly familiar investments will reduce uncertainty, whereas a persistent search for new and more promising investments will drastically increase uncertainty. All in all, then, it is not so much the medium of investment but rather the manner of approach to it which will determine the level of uncertainty for an investor.

UNCERTAINTY AND AROUSAL

Generally, uncertainty of any situation leads to heightened "arousal" (i.e., high mental alertness and physical activity). Arousal is a crucial ingredient of emotions like elation and excitement on the one hand and feelings like discomfort and distress on the other.

High arousal plus pleasure yield: excitement, elation, vigor, hope, happiness, power, creativity, boldness.

High arousal plus displeasure yield: discomfort, anxiety, distress, fear, disgust, anger, tension, panic, hate, cruelty, humiliation, pain, puzzlement.

One characteristic of high-uncertainty investments is that more often than not they generate unpleasant feelings because of the great burdens they impose on investors (i.e., financial demands such as negative cash flow, setbacks, or outright failures). There are of course those occasions of investment success which yield excitement, elation, and feelings of power and creativity. However, such experiences tend to be infrequent for most investors.

Thus, investment uncertainty more often results in feelings of the second group listed above (arousal plus displeasure) than in those of the first group (arousal plus pleasure). A simplified capsule summary of all this is that:

> *Level of investment uncertainty is directly proportional to degree of discomfort and anxiety (STRESS) for the investor.*

This principle explains why we are taking time with the concept of uncertainty. Assessing the uncertainty of an investment is extremely useful for anticipating our particular emotional reactions to it. Since stress is associated with anxiety, fear, discomfort, distress, worry, or tension, it is evident that high-uncertainty investments extract a heavy psychological toll from investors. And, as we shall see, for persons with certain types of temperament, these effects of stress are intolerable. Many an investor has lived with a highly uncertain type of investment for months or even years to finally "crack" under the strain, sell out at a loss, and thereafter watch in dismay as the investment eventually flourishes.

Knowing how much investment uncertainty each investor can tolerate—and this level is different for each temperament type—is extremely valuable in bracketing the types of investments we should consider and others we strictly should avoid.

The stress generated by high-uncertainty investments is not only harmful to the pocketbooks of those who are temperamentally unsuited to such investments, but it is harmful as well to the health of any and all persons who would take on these investments.

An extreme example of high-uncertainty investing is the in-house daily trading in stocks or commodities by large brokerage houses or financial institutions. Those who perform such jobs constantly have to be informed and be aware of extremely complex market forces and news events. Using computers on a minute-to-minute basis, they keep tabs on all news and events which affect the prices of stocks or commodities they trade. The complexity is immense because of the steady stream of information they must process. Change is ever present and often is unexpected. But, at least for the seasoned professional, the experience is familiar. Together, these factors make for exceedingly high uncertainty and associated high stress that few individuals can tolerate and live with successfully.

If on a scale of one to ten, the uncertainty of investing in an apartment building for the novice scores six, uncertainty for the in-house trader who actively trades millions of dollars worth of stocks or commodities each day is ten.

Remembering that such traders make million-dollar decisions regularly during the course of a day's work, it is seen that those who are unduly affected by stress are likely to perform poorly. They might fail to notice some crucial indicator or piece of news that affects a purchase they have made, react too slowly to an announcement from a company whose shares they own, or simply panic and act irrationally. Poor performance in this case could mean a loss of several hundred thousand dollars within an hour and one is not likely to keep such a job for long when these losses outweigh the gains.

A most dramatic illustration of the stresses associated with such exceedingly high-uncertainty investments is the fact that these traders (or financial gladiators) tend usually to be young—they do not last long enough health-wise or stamina-wise to grow old in the business.

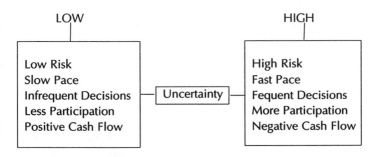

A DIFFERENT VIEW OF INVESTMENT UNCERTAINTY

An alternative, and perhaps more familiar, framework in which to define investment uncertainty relies on the concepts of *risk, pace, decision frequency, investor participation*, and *cash flow*.

"High-risk" investments usually involve changes (often rapid) and unexpected surprises that affect the worth of one's investment and usually require consideration of many complex factors which influence the investment. High risk, then, goes along with high uncertainty.

"Pace" refers to the speed of actions required of an investor to keep up with an investment. Pace of a savings account is near zero, that of a stock investor who trades once or twice a year is extremely slow, and that of a commodities trader who makes purchases and sales each day is exceedingly high. High pace involves fast decisions and responses to fast, and possibly unexpected, changes; thus, high pace means high uncertainty.

Your home which you may have purchased 16 years ago also is an investment. You probably have not made another decision regarding that investment since the date of purchase, except possibly the decision to keep it or to remodel. In contrast, if you purchase a stock and it moves up in price, you must decide whether you want to take profits by selling; if it moves down, you must decide whether it is likely to continue to plummet and therefore to sell, or decide that it will reverse direction and therefore to hold.

"Decision frequency" relates to pace and reflects the speed with which one must balance the pros and cons of two or more avenues of action and act upon a conclusion. Decisions involve active (and mentally alert) consideration of the complexities of various choices. Frequent decisions are necessitated by investments whose values are easily influenced by a great variety of circumstances and new developments, that is, changes and unexpected events. High decision frequency, like high pace, goes with high investment uncertainty.

For some investments, required participation of the investor is minimal. Supposing you purchase shares of a money market fund. Your participation is limited to the acts of purchase, and later sale, of the shares. No other actions are required. In contrast, the investor who purchases an apartment building and manages it herself participates regularly and actively, but not as actively as say one who trades stocks for his own account on a daily basis. The latter must keep up with general economic news, financial information, and technical data relevant to the stocks he trades. He must keep track actively of the stock quotes each day and decide on the opportune times to buy and sell. All this entails several hours of work each day just to take care of the investments.

"Participation," then, means dealing with the complexities, changes, and unexpected events associated with investments. More participation goes along with greater uncertainty of investment.

"Cash flow" refers to whether the investment generates cash (positive cash flow) or requires cash infusions (negative cash flow). Sometimes, in the case of negative cash flow, there is a sudden and unexpected demand for large funds to be added to the investment. In the case of savings-type accounts, the investor receives a steady stream of interest—cash flow is positive. A stock-oriented mutual fund which pays an aggregate stock dividend also involves positive cash flow. The apartment building, however, involves outlay of funds by the investor—negative cash flow—and this outlay may sometimes have to be large.

Negative cash flow can be drastic for the speculative investor in stocks or commodities. If she has borrowed money from her broker to purchase stocks or commodities (i.e., leveraged her investment) and there are adverse and rapid price moves, she receives a "margin or maintenance call," a notice to add funds to the account or else one or more of her holdings are sold, probably at a loss.

Negative cash flow requires regular or irregular personal-finance readjustments by investors. Even when the negative cash flow is on a fixed schedule and is expected, investors must make changes in their life patterns to set aside the required funds. When negative cash flow varies and sometimes is unexpectedly large, sudden and drastic financial adjustments are required of investors. It follows that negative cash flow increases uncertainty whereas positive cash flow reduces uncertainty.

The alternative criteria (risk, pace, decision frequency, investor participation, negative cash flow) help to define further the concept of investment uncertainty.

INVESTMENTS GRADED BROADLY ON UNCERTAINTY

To help "flesh out" the concept of uncertainty, it also is useful to list a number of common investments and order them roughly in terms of their uncertainty levels.

The group of lowest uncertainty investments consists of U.S. Treasury bills and notes and federally insured CDs and money market accounts at banks and savings institutions. When large sums are involved and exceed bank deposit insurance limits, uncertainty can be reduced through direct purchases of U.S. Treasury bills and notes.

A slightly higher-uncertainty group of investments also involves purchases of various interest-paying instruments such as corporate bonds, closed-end bond funds, municipal bonds, or U.S. Treasury bonds with distant maturity dates. If you purchase a corporate or U.S. Treasury bond which pays an 8 percent interest rate and is due in the year 2004, there is an increment to uncertainty because you may not be able to hold the bond until maturity. Needing the funds earlier, you may be forced to sell at the prevailing market value and this may be less than the payoff value of the bond if held to maturity.

Similarly, closed-end bond funds fluctuate in value depending on prevailing interest rates. Ten thousand dollars invested in such a fund when the prime is 11 percent would be worth more if the prime were to drop to 8 percent and would be worth considerably less with the prime at 19 percent. Thus, uncertainty for this second group of investments is increased by variations (changes) in prevailing interest rates, and thereby, changes in the value of the investment—as interest rates increase, one's capital shrinks, as they drop, one's capital appreciates.

Safety ratings of bonds are also important in determining uncertainty levels. High-safety corporate or municipal bonds (e.g., those rated double-A or triple-A) hardly ever involve unexpected and catastrophic surprises, such as the inability of a company or municipality to pay its debts. However, with low-safety instruments, chances of financial insolvency, and uncertainty, are greater.

Trust-deed loans made to others and secured by real property constitute the third group of slightly higher-uncertainty investments. Here again, if the trust deed cannot be held to maturity and must be sold at an earlier date, it usually is sold at a "discount" or loss. In addition, there is a greater element of risk in that the borrower may fail to make the loan payments, necessitating foreclosure. This unexpected change in the investment would require difficult financial adjustments from an investor and accounts for the greater uncertainty.

The fourth group includes stock mutual funds or other professionally managed funds which invest in real estate. With these, as in the case of bonds, investor participation is simply limited to the purchase, and eventual sale, of the instrument. The only changes during the course of investment are small variations in income and possibly large variations in the total value of the instrument. Gains or losses of capital make these investments more uncertain than those in the preceding groups.

Professionally managed stock funds differ in uncertainty depending on the objectives of the funds. Those which emphasize income and preservation of capital are, of course, lower in uncertainty than funds which invest aggressively for "growth" or to maximize capital gains. Others combine some of the features of "growth" and "income" by investing in preferred stocks or convertible bonds and thereby fall somewhere in between on uncertainty.

The fifth group includes oil and gas drilling ventures or equipment purchases and subsequent leases—also professionally managed. The difference between this and the preceding group of fund investments is that the present group of tax shelter programs may require additional infusions of capital from investors. Considering that an investor cannot clearly anticipate his financial situation a year or two later when he may have to make significant additions to invested capital, negative cash flow is a major additional source of uncertainty here.

There are also managed funds which invest in precious metal stocks. Other funds of yet greater uncertainty trade in commodities. Basically, it is possible to select from a wide range of uncertainty levels by simply investing in funds which are managed professionally. As we shall see, this tactic is most suited to a number of temperament types.

Higher levels of uncertainty are approached when investors directly take charge of investments, as in the case of individual purchases of real estate, stocks, or commodities. The particular level of uncertainty is determined with the criteria already mentioned. An apartment complex which is overseen totally for the investor by a management firm involves far less complexity, change, and novelty than one managed by the investor himself. Again, a stock portfolio which involves a few trades a year has fewer changes and novelty than one involving a few trades a week.

Thus, within any of the aforementioned categories of investment, the actual level of uncertainty is determined by complexity, variation, rate of change, unexpected events, and novelty. Real estate investments, in particular, can range across the broad gamut of uncertainty levels. For active investors who frequently buy, remodel, and sell real properties, most aspects of uncertainty are high (although still not as high as the uncertainty for an active stock or commodity trader). For the typical real-estate investor who purchases single family homes or small apartment buildings, uncertainty can be kept at a low level with the use of outside managers.

Bear in mind also that real estate values tend to change slowly. A ten percent change for a stock over the course of a week is not unusual, but such a change in value in real estate usually requires at least one year. The typical, and considerably slower, rates of change in real estate make this medium highly desirable for those whose temperaments are not suited to high-uncertainty investments.

Generally, the more ambitious an investor is in seeking high returns, the greater are the chances that investment activity will be more complex and involve unexpected, rapid changes and novelty.

However, high achievement goals and the associated high uncertainty and stress do not necessarily produce high returns. An investor may work extremely hard for several years and yet produce minimal gains easily attainable with a savings account; worse yet, he may achieve a net loss.

A main objective of this volume is to assist investors select levels of investment uncertainty with which they can live comfortably and profitably. One's temperament and one's particular life circumstances determine this maximum tolerable level of uncertainty. Different temperament types have differing levels of stress tolerance—and remember that uncertainty and stress levels are positively correlated. Similarly, certain life circumstances are highly stressful in themselves and our analysis will show that such conditions are not conducive to successful investing in high-uncertainty instruments.

Chapter 4

Pleasant-Unpleasant Temperament

Evelyn is a very intelligent woman holding a highly responsible position in a drug manufacturing company. To get as high up in the corporate world as she has, she has learned to camouflage her emotional and spontaneous reactions to situations. During the workday, she acts the part of a mature, unemotional business lady. Her relationships with coworkers are limited to work-related issues. She deliberately avoids any negative comments to, or about, others at work and keeps her many reservations about various individuals to herself. She has no close friends among the approximately twenty coworkers in her department. The only occasions when she socializes with others from work are the mandatory social affairs.

When Evelyn gets home from work, she cannot relax until she has spent an hour or more unburdening herself to her husband about the problems she encountered during her workday. On the rare occasions when they socialize, their companions tend to be her husband's friends. Evelyn does not hug, kiss, or touch others during greetings. She often comments negatively on persons, actions, or events when social meetings break up and when she is again alone with her husband.

UNPLEASANT TEMPERAMENT

The preceding sketch of Evelyn's characteristic ways of relating to persons and situations reveals a definite bias toward an unpleasant temperament. The telltale sign of such a temperament is "negative social expectations." This means expecting that social interactions with others will not be fun, rewarding, or gratifying and expecting that such exchanges will be unsatisfying or even painful or punishing. The crucial quantity is the difference between the positive and the negative expectations. Compared with most persons, Evelyn's positive expectations are low and her negative expectations are high. We thus consider her temperament to be unpleasant.

Expectations are at the core of a well-defined sequence of actions and reactions which reinforce and maintain the expectations. If one expects to be dissatisfied or even hurt, it is difficult to be outgoing, helpful, cheerful, and sociable with others. So, someone who has generally negative expectations is less likely to act in a friendly and pleasant way when encountering strangers or acquaintances. Others, in turn, reciprocate the coldness, unpleasantness, or disagreeableness. A person such as Evelyn who is cold and aloof with others probably elicits distant and less friendly reactions from those she meets. These reactions in turn confirm and reinforce her generally negative expectations—that is, being with others is not fun and can be uncomfortable and even painful.

A vicious cycle is formed and maintained with negative social expectations at its core. Negative expectations result in less pleasant or more negative reactions to others; others reciprocate accordingly, thus confirming the expectations.

Negative social expectations are part of a broader pattern of negative expectations about life in general, commonly referred to as pessimism. The opposite end is positive social expectations forming the core of generally

Figure 4-1   The Vicious Cycle of Negative Expectations

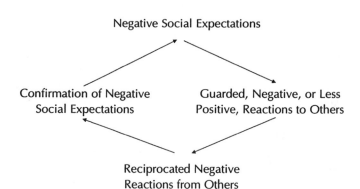

positive expectations in everyday life and referred to as optimism.

Persons who have an unpleasant temperament also have a tendency to view life with a bleak and negative outlook. Depending on other characteristics of temperament associated with unpleasantness, this negative outlook may be infused with feelings of helplessness and despair; it may consist of problem-ridden ruminations and preoccupation with upsetting and disturbing events exaggerated out of proportion; it may involve anger, disgust, irritation, and frustration with others and life events; or it may be a calmer variant of the latter in which the individual feels removed from, and unconcerned with, others and situations because these seem uninteresting, boring, or mundane.

Sometimes an unpleasant temperament is difficult to detect. George seems sociable enough. He has several friends and is close to various members of his family. However, if you were to get to know him, you would find that George's topics of conversation typically have a negative tone. Examples are the problems he is having in a class because his professor will not let him make up an exam he missed, a headache he gets regularly which will not go away no matter how much aspirin he takes, losing a whole stack of his books by forgetting them under a lunch table at the cafeteria, problems he is having with his roommate, his rear-ending of another car which is going to increase his insurance premiums, his inability to sleep during the week of exams, his worries about a career after graduation, or his concerns about the country's economy and politics.

George's social manner seems pleasant enough, but a sample of his conversation topics reveals a prevailing preoccupation with problems and generally unpleasant matters. Indeed, George's manner is not pleasant enough to alleviate the burden created by his choice of topics. George's unpleasant emotional state tends to affect negatively the moods of those who spend time with him. After a couple of hours in his company, visitors are left feeling fatigued, slightly unhappy, or even upset. Understandably, they avoid get-togethers with him without being able to pinpoint the reasons for such reluctance.

In addition to negative social expectations and general pessimism about life, negative topics of conversation thus provide an important source of clues about unpleasant temperament. We refer to someone as having an unpleasant temperament when, compared with others, the individual typically spends more time in one or more of a variety of unpleasant emotional states (including anxiety, anger, boredom or depression, and uncaring or unconcerned feelings).

PLEASANT TEMPERAMENT

It is easier to understand and detect an unpleasant temperament when we are also acquainted with its opposite, a pleasant one. Consider Patricia. She is usually in an almost manic state. When she is with friends, she talks rapidly about a variety of topics, she does not have any sense of reserve, fears of rejection, or deliberate and calculated mannerisms designed to have a "proper" or "socially appropriate" effect. She simply talks and behaves in ways which come naturally to her. She has an endless reservoir of jokes and it is hard to spend an evening with her without hearing some new ones. She calls friends at odd times just to talk and incidentally to mention one of her new jokes.

Patricia hardly ever asks her friends for favors, but readily volunteers to help with their problems, especially when these are in her areas of expertise. Helping a friend is a good excuse for Patricia to spend time socializing and being in the company of people, and having fun is at the top of her list of priorities. She is almost never anxious or worried, bored or depressed, and rarely shows signs of irritation or anger. Her companions, after they've spent time with her, feel a bit manic themselves—being with her is like getting an emotional boost.

Patricia has temperament qualities that are opposite to both Evelyn's and George's. In comparison with Evelyn, she has stronger positive social expectations and weaker negative ones. She expects get-togethers to be fun and rewarding, acts accordingly and draws out positive reactions from her companions or even strangers. These responses of others in turn serve to confirm and reinforce her positive expectations—thus creating a cycle of positive expectations, pleasant actions, others' reciprocating positive reactions, and more positive expectations.

Patricia is broadly optimistic—she views life in a positive and hopeful light, expecting most things to turn out well. Also, her topics of conversation, unlike George's, are elated, exciting, happy, and vigorous. Patricia, then, exemplifies one variant of pleasant temperament, the kind we will later describes as "exuberant."

Positive versus negative social expectations, more general optimism versus pessimism, and pleasant versus

Figure 4-2   The Beneficial Cycle of Positive Expectations

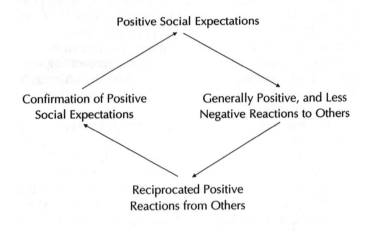

unpleasant conversation topics are major components of pleasant versus unpleasant temperament, respectively.

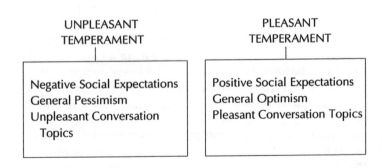

NONVERBAL AND SUBTLE CLUES TO PLEASANT-UNPLEASANT TEMPERAMENT

There are many other specific clues to pleasant and unpleasant emotions, and thereby to temperament. Facial and vocal expressions are two of the more important among these. Smiles, laughter, or generally happy expressions imply pleasure, as do jovial and elated voice quality. Frowning, glaring, angry, disgusted, crying, fearful, sneering, smirking, or mocking facial expressions and unhappy, sad, disgusted, or angry voice in turn imply displeasure. When the pleasant (unpleasant) cues predominate in a person's social manner, it adds weight to the inference of a pleasant (unpleasant) temperament.

Although the face and voice are centrally important means of conveying pleasant-unpleasant feelings, their value in detecting temperament is diminished since there is heightened awareness of such expressions and these can be modified readily to camouflage true feelings. This is why some of the less obvious indicators of pleasure-displeasure which are based on verbal contents of conversation tend to be more useful.

Aside from pleasant versus unpleasant conversation topics as subtle indicators, there is the frequency of complaints, criticisms, and disagreements. Someone who usually complains about one thing or another, criticizes this or that, or expresses disagreement rather than agreement during conversations, reveals an underlying streak of unpleasant temperament.

Contrasting qualities of contentment, praise, or agreeableness underscore pleasantness of temperament. For example, pleasant individuals agree often and like to communicate this agreement by pointing out that they, too, have had similar experiences to those of their conversational partners. They frequently use expressions such as "uh-huh," "definitely," "me, too," "same here," or "I agree," conveying a generally positive disposition.

Several qualities of speech and voice which have nothing to do with what is said are also helpful to identify pleasant-unpleasant feelings. A high frequency of "speech errors" indicates anxiety or discomfort and, therefore, displeasure. Examples of speech errors are sentence corrections where the speaker interrupts mid-sentence to correct or paraphrase uncompleted sentences, stuttering, slips of the tongue, intrusions of unrecognizable or incoherent sounds, omissions where parts of words or entire words are omitted, or unnecessary repetitions of words within a sentence.

A related speech characteristic is the "halting or hesitating quality of speech." This is a pattern of speech lacking steady tempo or fluency; it tends to start and stop unexpectedly and gives the impression of undue effort or labor in producing speech.

We all tend on occasion to produce more speech errors or to exhibit a more halting or labored speech due to temporary high levels of discomfort or anxiety. These speech aberrations provide yet another clue to unpleasant temperament only when they are a general characteristic of a person's speaking style. Finally, voice tremor indicates tension. When such tremor usually accompanies a person's speech, it implies characteristic anxiety or tension and, therefore, displeasure.

To sum up, there are several clues which we can use to identify the pleasantness-unpleasantness of a person's temperament. Among these, positive and negative social expectations, positive and negative topics of conversation, and general optimism and pessimism are the most important. The pleasant-unpleasant qualities of face and voice, frequencies of agreement versus disagreement, praise versus criticism, rejoicing versus complaint, statements regarding similarities with conversation partners, speech errors, halting or labored speech, and voice tremor are some of the remaining important clues to pleasant-unpleasant feelings.

We infer pleasant temperament when various indicators of pleasant feelings occur frequently—more often than they occur in others. Similarly, we infer unpleasant temperament when the clues to unpleasant feelings are unusually frequent.

Specifically, to infer the pleasantness-unpleasantness of someone's temperament, first you need to focus on their social expectations and also form some mental average of the pleasantness-unpleasantness of their conversation topics. If these two important indicators together point in one or the other direction, chances are you can safely base your inference on these two alone.

There are, of course, many instances where the individual does not clearly reveal either extreme. An observation of someone over a period of weeks is likely to reveal a mixture of pleasant and unpleasant clues at different times. Nevertheless, one or the other group of indicators usually prevails across a variety of situations. The degree to which the pleasant or unpleasant set predominates provides an estimate of the strength of that quality.

There is one important class of individuals for whom pleasant-unpleasant social expectations need to be given less weight in evaluating pleasantness of temperament. These are first- or second-generation immigrants from countries where old cultural traditions emphasize close family ties and an extended network of stable and highly interdependent social relationships.

For immigrants from the countries of the Middle East, Orient, or South America, for example, positive and negative social expectations are difficult to pinpoint correctly because their outward behavior gives the appearance of friendliness and enjoyment of close relationships with their families and many friends. Nevertheless, significant numbers of such individuals, while complying with culturally inbred traditions of emphasis on close and highly interdependent social ties, reveal the qualities of unpleasant temperament via some of the other cues mentioned. Therefore, greater reliance should be placed on pleasantness-unpleasantness of conversation topics and some of the other verbal and nonverbal clues in inferring the temperament of such individuals.

PLEASANTNESS-UNPLEASANTNESS AND INVESTMENTS

We are now prepared to apply our understanding of pleasant versus unpleasant temperament to the arena of investments. In Chapter 3, we categorized investments along the dimension of "uncertainty." Complex, varied, rapidly changing, unexpected, and novel qualities of investments contribute to high uncertainty, whereas simple, stable, slowly changing, expected, and familiar qualities characterize low-uncertainty investments.

The greater the uncertainty of an investment, the more is the stress and anxiety for the investor. This principle which applies to all investors is modified somewhat depending on investor temperament.

Pleasant investor temperament attenuates the stress effects of uncertain investments; it does not eliminate the stress and anxiety created by such investments, but reduces these somewhat. In contrast, *unpleasant investor temperament accentuates and aggravates these stress effects.*

Obvious implications are that those with pleasant temperaments are better able than the average person to tolerate, live with, and cope successfully with, high-uncertainty investments. Since high uncertainty also means high risk, fast pace, rapid decision frequency, frequent and active investor participation in the investment, and negative cash flow, persons with pleasant temperaments do better at investments which have one or more of these characteristics.

Parallel implications for those with unpleasant temperaments are that they are prone to have more difficulty than the average person with high-uncertainty investments. Specifically, this means they are likely to respond with greater anxiety, fear, discomfort, frustration, anger, or even terror or panic, and their investment decisions are going to be affected adversely by such emotions.

CASE EXAMPLES

Supposing Martha who has an unpleasant temperament uses a significant part of her cash savings to purchase a stock or a bond and soon thereafter is confronted with a 15 percent paper loss (meaning the value of the stock or bond drops 15 percent but Martha does not actually have a loss unless she sells). At this point, Martha is emotionally past the stage of discomfort or frustration and well into fear. Adverse news in a major financial paper or magazine relating to the company she has invested in or even some supposedly negative economic development is apt to accentuate this fear. As it is, she spends a good deal of time (time, by the way, which could be put to use more profitably practicing her profession) worrying about her loss. She sees the situation getting much worse and the added piece of bad news looks like the trigger for one more decline.

Martha spends half the night awake, absolutely miserable, calls her broker in the morning, and without any consultation, asks him to sell her stock or bond. She figures that she is better off with a 15 percent, than with a 30 percent or even 50 percent, loss which she is convinced is what will happen if she holds on.

What has happened is that the adverse news drives Martha to her emotional breakpoint and to capitulation: she has been nudged over from fear into terror and she simply wants out of an intolerable emotional situation. Her decision to sell is not based on the facts and realities of the investment, but rather is motivated strictly by emotional demands. And, indeed, when Martha gives her order to sell, she takes a deep sigh of relief—she feels as though a heavy burden has suddenly been lifted off her. She is glad to take the loss just to gain relief from intolerable pain.

What happens to the investment next is anyone's guess. The stock or bond may recover its lost value or continue to deteriorate. But, the point is that Martha was unable to make rational judgments based on factual information about the future of her investment.

More importantly, she was unable to follow through on her investment game plan. Prior to investing a significant portion of her cash, she must have spent considerable time and effort in making the particular selection and she probably made that decision under far more favorable and calmer emotional circumstances. Thus, the initial move was more likely to have been a rational one and such a move usually involves a plan.

The plan, for instance, may have been to hold the investment for several years. In case of a bond purchase, the plan may have been to hold the bond until a period of lower interest rates, thus almost guaranteeing return of capital and continued interest income. In case of a stock purchase, the plan may have been based on future promise of a particular company within a lively and vigorous segment of the economy. This or any other similar plan which had been made under calm, considered, and favorable circumstances was forgotten during those endless days of fear. During the crisis, Martha's emotions took center stage. Lacking a positive and optimistic perspective, she focused unduly on the negative developments and failed to gain sufficient distance from the latter to view them within the broader and more balanced perspective of her investment plan.

Consider what might have happened if Caroline who has a pleasant temperament had found herself in the same investment predicament. Caroline would have been far less likely to become overly preoccupied with the 15 percent paper loss of capital. Life for Caroline includes many positive and happy elements and it would be difficult for her to turn from all of those and to focus almost exclusively on any small aspect with a lot of negatives. Caroline has an in-built balancing mechanism which helps her maintain a proportioned perspective of a difficult situation within the context of the rest of her activities and circumstances.

True, the paper loss would probably have been a source of discomfort and frustration, because Caroline also would have been aware that her plan did not seem to be working. However, being positive, Caroline would recognize that temporary reversals occur with most plans and it pays to be hopeful and persistent and to adhere to something which one has put into effect with some care.

Given this more balanced perspective and essentially stronger emotional condition, it would be difficult to throw Caroline entirely off balance and into a state of frenzy with any single piece of bad news either about the company or the economy. Indeed, being the sociable type she is, she would probably talk freely about her investment with friends and experts and receive varied information and advise about how to deal with it. Being positively inclined, she would be likely to remember and consider the positive analyses of her situation. In this way, she would be far more likely to adhere to her rationally devised plan of investment action. Thus, Caroline's chances of ultimate success would be greater than Martha's because her investment actions would be more in line with realistic and rationally planned, instead of emotional, considerations.

GENERAL CONSIDERATIONS

The examples of Martha as having an unpleasant, and Caroline as having a pleasant, temperament and their respective manners of handling a difficult investment situation only provide a limited view of the effects of pleasant-unpleasant temperament on investments. For a complete picture, we need the remaining two major dimensions of temperament, because the way a person reacts to high-uncertainty investments depends also on how they rate on those two dimensions. Actually, there are several types of pleasant, and separately, of unpleasant temperament and each of these copes in a distinctive manner with uncertain investments.

With the information given so far, it is nevertheless possible to abstract some of the general characteristics associated with pleasant and unpleasant temperaments. Life for someone with a pleasant temperament includes many positive and happy elements, and it is difficult for such a person to focus almost exclusively on negative developments in investments. Thus, although reversals and paper losses are still a source of discomfort and frustration, such persons recognize that temporary reversals occur with most plans. They are not likely to be thrown off entirely, or worse yet, get into a state of terror with any single piece of bad news or any adverse development. Instead, being generally hopeful, they possess a positive and constructive attitude toward their investments and are likely to persist and to adhere to their plans.

Indeed, one problem inexperienced pleasant individuals may have with investments is due to their optimism. Such optimism may lead them more often than is justified to assume a bullish investment stance and to fail to recognize adverse markets or to take advantage of short positions in such markets. With experience, however, some pleasant types, particularly the relaxed and docile, can learn to overcome this over-optimistic bias in investing.

In comparison, those with unpleasant temperaments, who tend to be generally pessimistic, are likely to latch onto bad news or negative developments with their investments. They worry, get anxious, or are even terrified both by what actually happens and by what might go wrong. Such a negative perspective gets in the way of a reasoned approach to difficulties associated with investments. Often, the investment position is closed out with a loss just to gain relief from worry and anxiety. Even when an investment succeeds, worry about giving up the gain may result in a premature sale, thus preventing additional future profits. In sum, an unpleasant disposition makes it harder to adhere to a rational investment strategy—one often is tempted to ignore or discard a plan because short-term developments seem to disconfirm it.

So, if someone only knew the pleasantness of their temperament and had no additional information, they could rely on the following guideline:

> *A pleasant temperament attenuates the stress effects of uncertain investments; in contrast, an unpleasant temperament accentuates and aggravates these stress effects.*

In making investment choices, persons with unpleasant temperaments would do better to select from among low-uncertainty investments—those which involve low risk, a slow pace, infrequent necessity for decisions, infrequent investor participation, and positive, rather than negative, cash flow.

Chapter 5

Arousable-Unarousable Temperament

Henry is an engineer. Ever since his childhood, he discovered it was extremely difficult for him to concentrate or study with the slightest amount of noise or other distraction. Even florescent lights with their steady humming sound make it difficult for him to think out a problem clearly.

At his office, he keeps the door closed while working, because footsteps in the corridor or conversation down the hall irritate him. He is the kind of person who picks up the phone on the first ring because the ringing is too disturbing to him. He abhors turmoil and interruptions.

Although he can work effectively and at a very rapid pace when his place of work is quiet and calm, his performance drops dramatically when there are distractions such as noise or conversation in the hall, when people drop in and interrupt his train of thought, or when he has a headache or is upset about some problem outside work.

At home, relaxation and comfort are of paramount importance to Henry. He is single and bought his house with two major criteria in mind—privacy and a quiet neighborhood. Over the years, he has reshaped his home into a functional, peaceful, and highly convenient environment. For example, he will not answer the phone prior to, during, and an hour after dinner. His telephone can be set so there is no audible ring and his phone-answering machine picks up immediately. When he is done eating and has had a chance to relax, he checks his messages and answers them selectively.

If he is awakened at night by any kind of disturbance or noise, it takes him at least half an hour to go back to sleep. And, any serious problem can be highly disturbing to him. He cannot simply ignore a problem and take care of other important things. He continues to be affected by the problem and ruminates about it, even dreams about it, until he has somehow resolved it.

Henry has what we'll refer to as an "arousable" temperament. To understand this concept, we need first to consider "arousal" which refers to a combination of physical activity and mental alertness.

AROUSAL

We distinguish emotions (which are transitory states) from temperament which is a lasting and stable attribute of the individual. To understand and describe temperament, we must examine a person's emotional states across a diverse and representative sample of everyday situations.

"Arousal" is one of three dimensions of state which we use to understand emotions—the other two are pleasure-displeasure and dominance-submissiveness. *A person's arousal level is the sum of his level of mental alertness and degree of physical activity*. In comparison, a person's level of arousability can be ascertained only by examining his arousal in different situations. This is the reason for our need to examine "arousal" first.

Sleep is a low-arousal state where we are mentally and physically inactive. Reclining and daydreaming in a chair is a slightly more aroused state. Reading a book intently involves even greater arousal since we are posturally more tense and mentally more active while being intent. Jogging is yet a higher state of arousal in that physical activity is great but mental activity remains low. A competitive sport requires very high levels of arousal, since players usually are physically very active and need to be mentally alert to plan game strategies.

Some physiological indicators of high arousal are EEG desynchronization (which refers to fast EEG activity and simultaneous decrease in alpha waves) and pupillary dilation.

Physical activity or exertion involves muscle tension, rapid rates of respiration, high blood pressure and its associated high pulse rate, perspiration, and high skin temperature. Thus, other bodily clues to high arousal are high oxygen consumption or rapid respiratory activity, high pulse rate, greater muscle tension, and in extreme cases, trembling or tremor, higher palmar sweating (GSR), and higher skin temperature.

Some of these same indicators come into play when an individual is simply seated but tense, excited, or intensely involved in some mental activity. In such instances, we again observe greater muscle tonus, faster pulse, or more perspiration. For instance, even during a conversation, you will note that a shift in posture from a reclining position to a forward-leaning one involves greater muscle tension in the midsection and that such a position shift is usually associated with more interest in the conversation or a desire to emphasize a point—both conditions involving greater alertness.

Arousal is a basic element of variable emotional reactions to situations and characterizes "states," that is, our transitory and short-lived conditions. Obviously, then, arousal cannot be used to describe a stable characteristic of a person such as that person's temperament. Instead, we use the concept of "arousable-unarousable" temperament to refer to a person's characteristic arousal reactions to high uncertainty (complex, changing, unexpected, novel) situations.

AROUSABILITY

We all react with a sharp increase in arousal when suddenly confronted with an increase in uncertainty—walking into a room full of strangers, being bumped by a pedestrian while walking on the sidewalk, a sonic boom, a friend becoming extremely emotional, skidding while driving, getting bad or good news about an investment, being interrupted in an important train of thought, having to select one of two different product brands quickly, or having the electricity go off at night. All these examples involve a sudden increase in complexity, a change, an unexpected happening, and/or something novel.

We respond to all such increases in uncertainty with a sharp rise in arousal followed by a gradual drop in arousal back to normal levels. The important differences for arousable, compared with unarousable, persons are that an "arousable" person has a larger than average increase in arousal and a slower than average drop in arousal back to normal levels. In contrast, an "unarousable" person shows a smaller increase in arousal and a faster drop back to normal.

Numerous occasions over the course of a day involve increases in uncertainty of the immediate situation. This means that an arousable person spends more time in high-arousal states than an unarousable one. Consider two persons, one arousable and the other unarousable, both going through the following daily schedule: a very hectic work day followed by a 30-minute commute to a grocery store in congested traffic, the crowded store with long waiting lines, the necessity of having to prepare a meal, and something going wrong while cooking. During all this, the arousable person is bound to be more aroused than the unarousable one.

It follows that some of the clues for identifying arousable persons are more frequent manifestations of high arousal. These consist of rapid and animated speech in loud volume; high degrees of facial expressiveness and gesticulation; pupillary dilation; in extreme cases, characteristic bodily tension accompanying highly restrained and stiff movements; signs of tension in speech evidenced by high frequencies of speech errors, halting speech, and particularly of voice tremor.

In contrast, unarousable persons are verbally and vocally less expressive—they talk at moderate paces with less varied intonation and with moderate volume. Their facial expressions and gestures are less varied and their bodily postures and movements evidence a more relaxed quality. Signs of tension in speech, such as errors, halting quality, and voice tremor are absent or less frequent. In extremely unarousable persons, speech is monotonous in intonation, soft in volume, and highly abbreviated—characterized by monosyllabic utterances. Also, postures and movements give an impression of low energy and lack muscle tonus (are limp).

Table 5–1 anticipates the analysis of how you can detect very high levels of arousability. The most important clue to this condition is tension in posture, movements, or quality of speech. Tension is a crucial component of extreme high-arousal states (e.g., the tension which accompanies extreme anger, terror, very high sexual arousal, extreme physical effort or exertion). Thus, the probability of tension in nonverbal behaviors and voice increases with greater arousal.

This role of tension during high arousal permits us to distinguish between nonverbal behaviors of arousable, compared with extremely arousable, individuals. Arousable persons appear volatile, mobile, full of energy, and expressive; whereas extremely arousable persons give the impression of restraint, low activity, infrequent, tense, and cautious speech, and restrained, tense, and stiff qualities of postures, movements, and overall manner. Extremely arousable individuals are, thus, distinguished from unarousable ones in terms of considerably greater restraint, caution, and tension in their general manner.

Table 5–1   Summary Clues to High and Low Arousability

Extremely Arousable:
   Restrained, inactive, tense, cautions, unexpressive manner
   Obvious tension in posture; rigidity of posture
   Stiff, almost mechanical, movements
   Speech tension, voice tremor, halting speech
   Socially withdrawn, loner, minimal conversation
   Schizoid

Arousable:
   Emotional, volatile, mobile, energetic, expressive
   Animated speech, expressive face, prone to gesturing
   High energy level in movements, speech, expressions
   Talkative
   Easily startled, jumpy

Unarousable:
   Unemotional, stable, moderately energetic and expressive
   Low expressiveness in face, movements, and gestures
   Slow and less inflected speech
   Not very talkative

Extremely Unarousable:
   Low energy in speech, movements, gestures, face
   Few movements, gestures, and facial expressions
   Limp or lax postures and movements
   Socially withdrawn, loner
   Soft speech volume, inexpressive and infrequent speech

Note: Do not expect to find all the clues together in the same person for each level of arousability. For instance, an extremely unarousable person may show the expected generally low level of energy in speech, movements, and facial expressions, but she may not be socially withdrawn and a loner. Basically, you want to look for a consistent pattern of clues from each cluster even though some of the clues may be lacking. Also, of course, remember that many individuals will fall somewhere in the middle of this dimension. For such persons, you will find a mixture of clues from both the arousable and unarousable ends of the dimension.

There is yet one more important way in which arousable and unarousable persons differ. We all respond to external sources of information (our surroundings, the persons in them, and events) as well as to internal information generated by memories and imagery relating to recent or long-past happenings. Compared with the unarousable, the arousable generate more information internally and thus increase the complexity of the overall (external plus internal) information which they must process. This, again, results in greater arousal for them.

Let us consider internally generated information briefly. These include occasions when we experience thoughts and mental images of situations or events which are apparently unrelated to what we are doing. You may be working at your desk and suddenly have the image of a specific past experience at a European restaurant pop into your head. The image can be vivid, recalling many details of the restaurant, your companions, your state of mind, and the food you had on the occasion.

More commonly, our internally generated information relates to memories of recent events and important emotional episodes in our day-to-day lives. You may repeatedly recall an uncomfortable social scene from the previous day or you may remember with pride your special accomplishment at work the previous week.

Thoughts and imagery which relate in obvious ways to recent events (or even memories and imagery of very distant, past events apparently unrelated to our current situation or actions) can be a very rich source of materials in our day-to-day psychological existence.

The frequency and intensity of such memories or imagery (that is, internally generated information) differs for arousable and unarousable persons. When the arousable experience an emotionally-charged and intense experience (such as a quarrel, a near-miss accident, an exciting sexual experience, a memorable meal, great success or failure at work), they tend to relive the experience frequently and with an intensity approaching the origi-

---

Table 5–2   More Clues to High and Low Arousability

Arousable

1. A tendency to frequently generate internal information. Such information is in the form of recalls of recent emotionally-charged events. It also consists of sudden and unexpected intrusions of long-past experiences in the form of visual imagery and/or recollections.
2. Inability to set aside an emotional experience and to go on with the rest of life.
3. Intense, complex, and emotional experiences become "psychological baggage"—the arousable person carries this baggage around while trying to deal with new, everyday problems, including the uncertainty of investments.

Unarousable

1. Less frequent intrusions of internally generated information into everyday activities.
2. Better ability to set aside emotional experiences and to go on with other things.
3. Less "psychological baggage" to carry around and therefore greater ability to cope with other complex, variable, rapidly changing, unexpected, or novel situations (including high-uncertainty investments).

---

nal experience. Although less arousable persons also remember such important experiences, the intensity of emotion during recall, and the frequency with which such events are recalled, is less. In short, *intense, complex, and emotional experiences are more likely to become psychological baggage for the arousable than for the unarousable and, thus, to generate information and arousal for them.*

You now know most of the clues to high and low arousability. When you know whether someone is arousable or unarousable, you can understand their reactions to investments that are high in uncertainty.

Since, as we have noted before, high-uncertainty investments generally tend to have more unpleasant than pleasant effects, this means they tend to elicit feelings of discomfort or anxiety. Alternatively, they elicit feelings of irritation or anger. The difference between these two sets of feelings is that displeasure and high arousal are combined with "submissiveness" (a feeling of lack of control) in the first, whereas displeasure and high arousal are combined with "dominance" (a feeling of having control) in the second.

Combinations of displeasure, high arousal, and submissiveness yield: discomfort, frustration, anxiety, fear, panic, terror.

Combinations of displeasure, high arousal, and dominance yield: irritation, disdain, aggression, disgust, annoyance, anger, hate.

For either of the two sets of emotions listed, reactions of arousable persons are more extreme than those of unarousable ones. Thus, when situations are uncertain and unpleasant, they are preferred less (disliked and avoided more) by arousable, than by unarousable, persons.

BACK TO OUR EXAMPLE—HENRY AND HIS INVESTMENTS

With this background, let us reconsider Henry and understand the reasons for his various preferences at work and at home. Complex mental work involves consideration of many components of a situation. It necessitates mental creation of hypothetical arrangements of parts of a situation and tests to see which arrangement yields a desired end result. This mental juggling act is full of changes, unexpected barriers, and novel challenges. Together with the associated complexity, it involves considerable uncertainty and is, therefore, arousing for all of us. Arousable persons such as Henry react to such work with even higher arousal than the average individual.

Situations or stimuli which induce high arousal and displeasure are avoided generally by most, particularly by arousable persons like Henry. This is why he could not study as a child when, in addition to his work, he had to contend with noise or distraction (i.e., unpleasant and arousing stimuli). His difficulties with humming fluorescent lights, his desire to keep his office door closed so as to reduce noise, or his quick response to a ringing phone are all similarly explained—he strongly avoids unpleasant and arousing stimuli since he responds to these with greater arousal than most. Turmoil and interruptions also involve displeasure and high arousal to which Henry shows the expected avoidance.

When unpleasantness and uncertainty increase and are unavoidable (overly hot or cold air, conversation of others, visitors who interrupt his train of thought, pain or physical discomfort, or any other problem) Henry's work performance deteriorates. This is because he, like all arousable persons, has difficulty coping with and functioning adequately in such situations.

Understandably, then, Henry selected his home to have privacy and quiet to yield low uncertainty. He redesigned the interior to achieve a peaceful, functional, and convenient atmosphere; that is, an atmosphere which is pleasant and low in uncertainty. Finally, we note that when Henry's arousal level is increased sharply (as when he is awakened at night or when he is preoccupied with a serious problem) it takes him a long time to get back to a relaxed, low-arousal state—again a characteristic of highly arousable persons. Also, being arousable, Henry generates internal information. He frequently recalls emotional events and such intrusions of past emotional experiences can be a distraction and a handicap in dealing with uncertainty.

Pleasant-unpleasant and arousable-unarousable qualities are two of the three basic dimensions of temperament. These characteristics are independent of one another so that we can have pleasant and arousable, pleasant and unarousable, unpleasant and arousable, and unpleasant and unarousable types of individuals.

Henry's reclusive work habits and socially isolated life style clearly show he is not outgoing, friendly, or sociable. On this basis alone, we can infer that he also has an unpleasant temperament. This explains his rather extreme avoidance of all categories of unpleasant and high-uncertainty situations, since qualities of his temperament combine with and exacerbate the unpleasant and arousing effects of these situations.

Imagine now what would happen if Henry were to get involved in a high-uncertainty investment. Let us say he has somehow entered the fast-paced and high-risk commodities markets. His interest is silver because, being an engineer, he feels he can relate to a commodity which is used mostly for industrial purposes. Since he likes to approach problems in a logical way, he appreciates the supply and demand situation in silver. He believes industrial demand is catching up with supply, which in turn means price of the metal is bound to rise.

Silver trades in 5,000 ounce contracts and assuming the metal trades at around $12.00 per ounce, each contract is worth $60,000. Henry has purchased two contracts for delivery six months out. That is, even though the silver is worth exactly $12.00 per ounce today, with the purchase of two contracts, he is entitled to 10,000 ounces of silver at $12.00 per ounce in six months from now. Henry has actually purchased two contracts worth a total of $130,000 (which includes $10,000 of interest) but has only used $13,000 from his savings account as a deposit.

It is this "leverage" (control of a high-priced investment with a small percentage of the value required as downpayment) that makes his investment highly uncertain. If silver moves up in price by 10 percent within a week after the purchase of the contracts—and this can happen easily in the commodities markets—then Henry will make $12,000, almost doubling his investment. If, on the other hand, silver were to lose 10 percent of its value in a short period of time, then Henry would lose almost his entire investment.

Actually, it is not unusual for silver to have a 2.5 percent fluctuation in value in the course of a few trading days. Such a fluctuation means a gain or a loss of $3,000 in a short period. To the novice, and Henry certainly is one, the commodities markets are capable of generating tremendously varied emotional experiences ranging from excitement, elation, pride, and feelings of power or mastery, on to discomfort, tension, anxiety, sleeplessness, panic, and absolute terror.

The market in silver is highly complex because there are many elements of our economy, the world economy, and world politics which influence price moves in silver. For instance, when interest rates rise, this generally has a dampening effect on prices of commodities such as silver, gold, and platinum. A crisis in the Middle East which threatens to reduce the supply of oil to the West usually drives prices up. Inflation, of course, increases prices of precious metals, whereas deflation and economic stability have an adverse effect on these prices. Finally, the decision of the U.S. Federal government or some other government to sell a part of its silver hoard on the open market can affect prices adversely.

These are only a few of the factors which influence silver prices; there are numerous others. Thus, altogether, a great many events and relationships affect the price of the metal. Aside from this great complexity, there are many changes (e.g., rapid and often unexpected changes in world events which affect prices). In Henry's case, there

also is novelty, because he is unfamiliar with the investment medium. So, the five components of high uncertainty (complexity, variation, rapid change, unexpected
events, novelty) are present and, since each component
is very strong, the uncertainty value of this investment
is tremendously high.

Uncertainty generates arousal. Also, depending on
whether changes in an investment are beneficial or harmful, there are added feelings of pleasure or displeasure,
respectively. Considering that prices do not move up or
down in a straight line, but rather backtrack and zig-zag
in often seemingly inexplicable ways, Henry is going to
be right only about half the time. This means during half
the time when prices move adversely, he will feel high
arousal and displeasure.

Remember that Henry is disturbed by slightly unpleasant and arousing events such as a telephone ring,
slightly hot or cold temperatures, or an interrupted job.
Since he cannot tolerate even such mild sources of discomfort and irritation, he has painstakingly arranged his
work and home life to eliminate these. You can imagine,
then, his psychological state when he is confronted frequently and unavoidably with extreme uncertainty and
displeasure from his investment over a course of weeks
or months.

It is safe to say that this investment is bound to be
a massive disaster for Henry. His unpleasant and arousable qualities will magnify the negative emotional impacts of his investment to the point where he frequently
will feel a vague sense of discomfort, be irritable, have
sleepless nights, be unable to concentrate at work, and
have his productivity plummet. He will also become even
more reclusive, begin to manifest psychosomatic symptoms such as headaches, nausea, feelings of exhaustion
or lack of energy, digestive irregularities, or respiratory
problems.

During periods when adverse price moves are rapid
and large, Henry will be frantic with fear and almost

totally unable to cope with his everyday life at work and at home. The stress generated by his investment will have a massive and highly negative psychological impact to the point that Henry will begin to suffer from one or more physical ailments. He will "crack," probably after experiencing several consecutive bad days. He will sell at any price within a period of a month or two, just to get out from under the strain. And, it will probably take him several months to overcome the adverse psychological and physical effects of the investment.

In terms of his temperament, Henry has two strikes against him in taking on higher-uncertainty investments. As we have already seen, persons with an unpleasant temperament are better off with low-uncertainty investments. Similarly, arousable persons are also much better off with investments that involve low uncertainty. In Henry's case, one who has both these attributes, low-uncertainty investments are *de rigueur*. The very first group of lowest uncertainty investments listed in our "Investment Uncertainty" chapter is more his cup of tea—savings accounts, U.S. Treasury bills or bonds, and money market funds. He can live comfortably with such investments and channel his energies and abilities in his profession.

MICHAEL—THE UNAROUSABLE

As a contrast to Henry, we need an example of an unarousable person, and Michael provides an interesting variation of this pattern. He reacts calmly and with deliberation during critical and highly stressful periods of his life. He works as a real estate agent and specializes in complex commercial transactions. Whereas most agents find it a handful to deal with one buyer and one seller in a single transaction, Michael enjoys dealing with two or more on each side of the transaction, juggling many pieces simultaneously and working frantically to hold these up in the air.

For example, he once entered escrow to buy a six-unit apartment building for not one, but six buyers. The plan was for each of the six to become owner-tenants of one unit apiece. Michael actually entered escrow with four possible buyers, hoping to keep the four and find two more to complete the transaction. This was only a small fraction of the uncertainty caused by dealing with six individuals, each with their particular financial and psychological problems and requirements, and trying somehow to create a workable and harmonious group out of it all. There were problems when one of the buyers dropping out, another failed to qualify financially, buyers disagreed on who got which unit, or disagreed on the terms of purchase. Michael had to solve each problem and keep the transaction from falling apart.

Michael usually manages to hold things together in other comparable situations. Despite fast-moving changes and unexpected hitches, he remains reasonably calm, keeps all important aspects of a purchase in proper perspective, decides on where it would be most beneficial to intervene, and acts according to plan.

In his own real estate investments, Michael usually is fascinated by complex situations which are so problematical as to be avoided by most. For example, he recently purchased a dilapidated house in a reasonably good neighborhood, paying essentially the price of the lot alone. He found a partner who was willing and able to remodel the house while living in it and who paid part of the mortgage expense for his share of the profits.

A few of the uncertainties in this arrangement were that his partner might have been unable to do all necessary repairs or pay his share of the mortgage payments during the two-year remodeling period. There could have been difficulties relating to material purchases, bookkeeping of expenses, and other financial controls and safeguards necessitated by any such partnership. Also, there might have been difficulty in agreeing about the sale price and terms once the house was ready to be sold.

Michael was undaunted by these complexities and possible adversities. He selected his partner carefully, entered into the arrangement and managed to see it through with a sizeable profit. At the end, he had one more contact he knew he could count on when other investment opportunities came along.

Michael's major strength in both his profession and his investing is his unarousable temperament. This quality has enabled him to develop the skills to deal effectively with complex and problem-laden situations avoided by most. Stress levels which ordinarily make others extremely uncomfortable and anxious are tolerable to Michael. He can work purposefully and rationally when confronted with highly complex and fast-paced events because low arousability attenuates his arousal (and therefore stress) to moderate levels in such situations.

Michael has discovered a niche in his profession and in investments which is uniquely suited to him and where he can be a formidable competitor. Importantly, his success in overcoming problems at various stages of a complex project helps to temporarily transform stress (displeasure and arousal) into excitement and elation (pleasure and arousal).

Unlike Henry, Michael is not troubled much by noise at work or at home. He lives easily with clutter and disorganization and prefers having several projects to work on simultaneously. Although he differs from Henry on arousability, he, like Henry, also has an unpleasant temperament. Michael works well with people but does not feel any particular warmth toward them. To him, others are like his cars—to be driven and steered in various directions and to be handled with care at critical junctures. He, too, has very few friends and lives alone. His primary gratifications in life come not from people but from the successes he achieves and from the fine material possessions he accumulates. Possibly, Michael's temperament is slightly more pleasant than Henry's, but the critical variable which determines their respective abilities to deal with uncertainty of investments is arousability. Henry's high arousability is a definite handicap whereas Michael's low arousability is an asset.

INVESTMENTS AND AROUSABILITY

An important difference between arousable investors like Henry and unarousable ones like Michael is that the emotional effects of investments permeate the everyday lives of the arousable, whereas the unarousable are better able to separate their investments from their work and family affairs. When investments of arousable persons do well, they feel happy and carry this over into their work situation and their dealings with their family. If, on the other hand, their investments do poorly, they are likely to be upset, agitated, morose, or angry and to have these emotions contaminate relationships with coworkers or family members.

Since high-uncertainty investments frequently exhibit dramatic shifts, the corresponding mood shifts of the arousable become a large drain on their abilities to relate to others and are an important source of interpersonal problems. In addition, the strong emotionality of the arousable can lead to inappropriate reliance on alcohol or drugs or contribute to a variety of physical ailments ranging from hypertension and associated cardiovascular problems, migraine headaches, ulcers, or respiratory illnesses, to name just a few.

In particular, actual, as distinct from paper, losses have a much stronger negative impact on the arousable than the unarousable. Such losses can cause the arousable great unhappiness for periods of days or weeks, persistent rumination, moodiness, and loss of sleep. In comparison, the unarousable more easily overcome a loss—they can deal with it objectively, forget it, and move on to other trades. The stronger emotional reaction of arousable persons to losses is yet another example of the psychological drain of uncertain investments for these investors.

It is possible to suggest appropriate investment areas when we have information only about a person's arousability and know nothing more about his or her status on the other two major dimensions of temperament. We know high uncertainty and low arousability are likely to yield success whereas high-uncertainty investments and high arousability are incompatible. Stated otherwise, *unarousable persons are better able to cope with higher-uncertainty investments that tend to generate discomfort, anxiety, and distress in all of us. In contrast, investment areas involving low, rather than high, levels of uncertainty are suited best for highly arousable individuals.*

There also are a few specific types of situations to which the arousable are highly vulnerable and which should be noted. Arousable persons have a strong tendency to make purchases when the news is good (and incidentally, prices are temporarily high) and to sell when the news is bad (with prices temporarily low). Supposing the investment medium of choice is the stock market or one of the futures markets where daily price fluctuations are common and in part are determined by various news events. An active trader in such markets generally can do better by buying on bad news and selling on good news. The arousable, however, are far more predisposed emotionally to do the opposite.

Good news, such as an unexpectedly positive earnings report of a company, creates feelings of pleasure plus high arousal and, for most individuals, naturally acts as a magnet for the shares of that company. The arousable feel this attraction even more than most others and, thus, are likely to act on it by making a purchase. Bad news, on the other hand, generates feelings of displeasure and high arousal, and leads to low preference or avoidance. Once again, for the arousable, this avoidance or repulsion is very strong and is likely to result in a sale if they happen to hold the news-related issue in their portfolios.

In short, *the arousable show more extreme swings of attraction, versus repulsion, toward an investment when it does well, versus badly, respectively.* In acting upon these emotionally determined swings, they have financially unfavorable outcomes. *In contrast, the unarousable are better equipped to resist these natural pushes and pulls of markets or even to act contrary to what, intuitively and emotionally, seems the natural thing to do.*

Another area where the arousable need especially be watchful is unusual, fast-paced markets. The stock market is useful in illustrating this point. The broad market usually moves slowly and gradually and generally is dull. However, on occasion, volume of transactions escalates suddenly and prices of many issues make large percentage up or down moves. In the same way, any individual issue has small and insignificant fluctuations in value with moderate transaction volumes for long periods of time. However, for occasional periods of a few days or a few weeks, the volume of trades in shares of a particular company increases suddenly and there are dramatic up or down moves in price.

Whether it is the entire market or a particular issue in which an investor is interested, it is important to remember that large movements and high volumes are conducive to high-arousal states. When price changes are rapid and favorable, pleasure and arousal from the events combine with an arousable temperament to generate high excitement and a desire for a highly active, fun-like pace. Under these circumstances, the arousable trade much too frequently, thus minimizing gains due to large commission and execution (bid versus ask) costs. When price moves are rapid and unfavorable, displeasure and arousal created by the market combine with an arousable temperament to generate high degrees of irritation or anger, or alternatively anxiety or fear. In such instances, the arousable act rashly and impulsively, responding mostly to their emotions while disregarding their longer-term strategies.

In brief, *fast-paced markets increase the emotional vulnerability of arousable persons*. Someone with this temperament may be able to overcome her emotional handicaps when markets are changing slowly and gradually, but lose her self-control in high-paced markets. Thus, the arousable need to diffuse the emotional impact of such markets by deliberately reducing their proximity to, or involvement with, these. They need to force themselves to turn to other activities and away from investments and to think about their investments at a distance and with more detached attitudes. For instance, watching the ticker tape and making trading decisions while doing so should be avoided strictly. Trading decisions should be made when the stock market is closed. This recommendation might be followed by the arousable in any case, even when markets are slow-paced. More generally, for the arousable, highly active markets automatically should ring warning bells!

MANAGED INVESTMENTS RECOMMENDED FOR THE AROUSABLE

One of the best ways for arousable persons to safeguard against temperament-driven investment losses is to rely on competent management of their funds. Fortunately for arousable individuals, there are widely available published ratings of performance records of investment funds and managers.

First, an investor must decide on the level of uncertainty with which she can live comfortably. Let us say she decides that savings accounts, although safe, do not provide a high enough rate of return and that a managed portfolio of corporate bonds is more appropriate. In this case, Moody's and Standard and Poor's provide carefully researched ratings of safety (and, therefore, uncertainty level) of individual bonds. The investor can next select a managed fund that specializes in corporate bond investments of very, or moderately, high-safety ratings.

Supposing, on the other hand, that an investor hoped for larger gains and were willing to chance the stock market. Here, again, there are numerous mutual funds which invest in stocks and whose investment records over the preceding six months, year, or five years are known. In fact, several research organizations regularly update and publish the top-performing mutual funds in each of these various time spans.

Another approach is to invest in managed syndications of real estate properties. Funds of many clients are pooled and residential complexes, office buildings, or shopping centers are either purchased outright or developed. Such real estate investments, equipment purchases and subsequent lease-backs, or oil and gas drilling programs, also offered by specialized companies or brokerage houses, often involve moderate or even low uncertainty. It is more difficult to obtain comparisons of performance records for these investment teams, although each management team probably has several ongoing projects initiated a few years earlier. Cash returns and tax advantages of the preceding programs can be analyzed to determine suitability of a particular program.

Remember that *less personal involvement with an investment reduces uncertainty*. If you personally administer an investment which is identical to one managed by a professional, the uncertainty is greater because of the necessity for you to be aware of, and cope with, all facets of the investment. In this sense, professionally managed accounts reduce uncertainty (and associated arousal), while attenuating the occasional excitement, thrill, and challenge provided by personal involvement. However, when personal involvement leads to unacceptable losses, it is far less expensive to have someone else profitably invest one's funds and then to use the proceeds to generate excitement elsewhere.

Chapter 6

Dominant-Submissive Temperament

Irene is an interior designer and is married to Jim who is nearly twenty years her senior. If you were to visit them at their home for dinner, you would find Irene in charge and taking a major role in guiding the conversation. Her husband, an attractive and quiet-mannered man, would tend to take on a supportive and less active role. Whereas Irene would address all her guests while speaking, Jim would show a definite preference for quiet and private conversations with only one person in the group.

Irene started work as an interior designer two years ago and already has moved into a special, top slot. She assists the proprietor, who having by-passed many other workers, relies on Irene for day-to-day business management. Some older workers resent the way Irene gradually usurped the choicest facilities and business opportunities at the office or her frequent suggestions about how to handle their exclusive clients. Younger workers find Irene's sense of confidence reassuring. They try to emulate, and benefit from, some of her aggressive business tactics.

Irene is relaxed and confident in dealing with others. She speaks loudly and clearly, with hardly any hesitation or speech errors. When she and her friends decide to go to a movie or to a restaurant, she does not balk at making suggestions and persists enough to get others to agree to her second, if not her first, choice.

She does not smile much during conversation, and reserves smiles for when she wants to establish rapport with someone or tries to influence others' actions. Similarly, while listening to others, she nods or says things like "uh-huh" infrequently, again reserving such gestures for special effect. Anyway, she would rather do the talking than encourage others in that role. In fact, she manages to take center stage in most social or work-related conversations.

Irene's husband, Jim, on the other hand, has worked at the same business office for decades. Although well-liked, Jim basically has held the same position without changes in responsibilities or status during the last twenty years. Jim has a diffident manner of relating to others, particularly with strangers or new acquaintances. At such times, his posture gives the impression of some tension. He permits others to lead the conversation and agrees frequently. In groups, he is relieved when others become the center of attention, allowing him to focus on one person he likes and knows well. His speech style often exhibits a slow, halting, and hesitant quality, giving the impression he is not certain about, can back up, or firmly believes in, what he says. People find it easy to interrupt Jim while he talks.

Jim is highly gratified with the way in which Irene selected their home, furnished it, and then organized their life together. He is glad to have her take charge of their children, the everyday business of running a household, and their social life. In short, Jim is happy to relinquish control in most areas of his family life to Irene whom he loves and trusts implicitly.

Jim has not had much success with his investments. His parents left him a moderate-sized inheritance consisting of stocks and bonds in a trust managed by a bank. Jim's father had been an officer of the bank. Knowing that his father's colleagues managed the trust somehow meant a lot to Jim. So, despite meager returns from these investments over a period of many years, Jim continued to rely on the same management and even added his personal savings to the same account.

His only worthwhile investment was the purchase of a house when he married Irene. It was Irene's insistence that they buy the finest home they could possibly afford which accounts for the large capital gain from this particular investment. Their home now easily is worth six to seven times the amount they paid for it in the mid-sixties.

In the mid-seventies, Irene could not help but notice the considerably higher prices paid for homes in their neighborhood. She visited homes that were for sale in the area and talked with realtors about real estate investments. She followed this up with a considerable amount of reading on the subject and became well-versed with the fundamentals of investing in this field.

By 1977, about a year and a half after her interest was sparked first, Irene was ready to act. She used $20,000 of her own savings and an additional $35,000 she borrowed from her father as downpayment on a twelve-unit apartment building in a good part of town. She made the purchase after a thorough search and aggressive negotiation. She estimated the purchase price of $265,000 to be about 5 percent below market value and felt comfortable with the projected income and expense statements.

Two years later, she could have sold the same building for almost twice the purchase price. Also, the rental income had increased enough to generate a respectable cash flow. Irene managed all facets of the investment and this indeed is how she became interested in interior design. Since her daughters were teenagers by then, she decided that she was ready to pursue a career of her own and joined the firm at which she presently works.

Irene's and Jim's approaches to socializing, work, and investments reveal diametrically opposite qualities of the dominant-submissive temperament continuum—Irene is dominant, Jim is submissive.

In general, a "dominant" individual controls, takes charge of, and influences other persons, events, and situations, whereas a "submissive" one tends to be controlled, influenced, and guided by others and by situations or circumstances.

A dominant temperament is conveyed by a social manner which implies strength, fearlessness, comfort, and relaxation; a submissive one is communicated with weakness, fearfulness, discomfort, and tension. Posture provides the clues to relaxation: upright position of torso and near symmetrical positioning of arms and legs show tension, whereas reclining or sideways-leaning position of torso and more asymmetrical placement of limbs indicate relaxation. Other clues to relaxation are rocking slowly while seated in a chair that permits such movements or leaning the head sideways or down.

In comparison with others, dominant persons talk more and tend to be the center of attention in social situations. They talk louder, generally without hesitation or halting speech, and smile and nod less often. (Smiling and nodding are signs of agreement with, or subservience to, conversational partners.) Dominant persons are prone to interrupt the speech of others mid-stream. They also readily express and act upon their evaluations of people, events, and places—not hesitating to say what they like or dislike, prefer or want, or to act in accordance with these evaluations and desires.

In contrast, submissive individuals talk less and softer; their speech is likely to be slow and halting or to involve errors and slips. In social situations, they relinquish the center stage to others and frequently smile and nod to show agreement. Submissive persons are reluctant to express their evaluations and desires or to act according to their likes and dislikes when such actions run counter to the opinions or wishes of others.

There are a large number of other psychological characteristics which distinguish dominant and submis-

Table 6–1

Dominant Social Manner

Appears strong, fearless, comfortable, and relaxed.

Talks more, readily expresses opinions, is evaluative, and easily becomes the center of attention.

Speech is louder, without hesitation; smiles and nods less in agreement.

Does not hesitate to interrupt the speech of others.

Table 6–2

Submissive Social Manner

Appears weak, apprehensive, timid, uncomfortable, and tense.

Talks less, is hesitant to express opinions or to disagree, and is uncomfortable being at center stage.

Speech is softer and can be hesitant; smiles and agrees frequently.

Is reluctant to interrupt others' speech.

sive persons. Tables 6–3 and 6–4 list a sampling of those characteristics. Please note that opposite qualities are not listed regularly. For example, under "submissive" we have the quality "shy," but the opposite, "outgoing" is not given under "dominant." You simply can infer the opposites as you read the tables.

Table 6–3

Dominant Psychological Characteristics

Readily makes decisions
Is noticeable in social situations
Is catered to by others
Shows initiative and originality at work
Can easily say, "no"
Tends to be critical
Is at ease in public speaking
Works out problems on own
Is willing to express opinions
Is confident in own abilities
Easily makes own choices
Is decisive
Has control over own emotions
Adheres to own convictions
Has control over own life situations
Has confidence in own ideas
Has control over others
Is a leader
Questions rules and regulations
Is confident in social situations
Is insistent on own rights
Puts self before others
Can inspire awe
Has self discipline
Can be vociferous
Is assertive
Is competent

INVESTING BY THE DOMINANT

Dominance is slightly favorable for success at high-uncertainty investments. However, compared with pleasantness and low arousability, beneficial effects of

Table 6–4

Submissive Psychological Characteristics

Is shy
Follows in group situations
Is hesitant to defend own opinions
Is uncomfortable when at the center of attention
Feels outside forces are in control of his/her life
Is intimidated by superiors
Needs emotional support from others
Wants others to make choices and decisions
Conforms to norms of peers
Relies on "experts"
Is susceptible to fads
Conforms to societal conventions
Relies on authority
Is willing to follow instructions
Is a follower
Follows rules and regulations
Is concerned with opinions of others
Is unwilling to disagree with others
Avoids confrontation
Is polite
Turns to others when faced with difficulties

dominance are more problematic and depend on the investor's two other temperament characteristics.

Dominant persons are likely to be achievement-oriented and ambitious, setting high and difficult goals. They are more likely than submissive persons to take risks in investing, to have self-confidence, and to follow through on their own investment judgements and strategies.

Dominant persons tend to make up their own minds about things after consultation with friends or professionals in investment fields or after study of the pertinent literature. They like to personally direct their investments or to do so indirectly through others subservient to them. Experts, news reports, or strong convictions of family or friends are not likely to sway dominant individuals from investment paths they select for themselves.

Such firmness of purpose can be both beneficial and harmful. It is beneficial when an investor has adequate technical preparation or consults with recognized experts in his selected investment field. When an investment plan is technically sound, carefully planned, and involves an analysis of probabilities of gains and losses, it is important for the investor to adhere to that plan and not be swayed by transitory events, news, or adverse conditions. A dominant person's sense of confidence, persistence, and firm purpose are of considerable value in this respect.

But, dominant individuals also tend to err in the direction of being overly stubborn and rigid in their investment strategies; unwilling to admit errors of judgement, inappropriateness of investment techniques, or even failure. In extreme cases, rigid adherence to preconceived notions without proper preparation and thorough study of the complexities of investments can have disastrous financial results. Despite inadequate technical preparation in the area in which they invest, some dominant persons may ignore alternative and more reasoned pathways suggested by investment literature or experts, continuing to believe in their strategies. Such rigidity may cause them to rationalize their failures up to a point where losses become overwhelming.

An additional trap for the dominant is their tendency to view investments as an arena of challenge or combat—to want to overpower invisible antagonists, the other traders, or simply to beat the market. In this way, some dominant persons (particularly those who also are arousable) tend to take on an overly combative approach to their investments. One group (described as "exuberant" in the following chapter) approaches trading the way it would approach sports or gambling. Another group (referred to as "hostile") has a tendency to want to butt heads with the market—to be overly antagonistic and unduly emotional in dealing with investments.

The achievement orientation, competitiveness, risk-taking, confidence, and ambition of dominant persons amplify effects of the remaining two qualities of temperament (pleasantness-unpleasantness and high versus low arousability) on investment success versus failure. Dominant persons, due to their ambition, are likely to select high-uncertainty investments since these provide a higher return on capital. But, success with such investments depends on other characteristics of a dominant individual.

When dominance is associated with impulsiveness, impatience, and poor planning, high-uncertainty investments result in great losses; when it is associated with deliberation, patience, and sound technical plans, investment benefits can be large.

In subsequent chapters, we will see how various combinations of dominance with pleasantness-unpleasantness and high versus low arousability yield characteristics of impulsiveness and impatience or opposites of these.

For now, it is important to emphasize that being dominant rather than submissive does not provide an investor with a strong psychological advantage. Unlike pleasantness of temperament which provides a clear advantage over unpleasantness of temperament and low arousability which is even a greater advantage over arousability in investing, dominance provides only a marginal advantage over submissiveness. Dominance only provides a strong advantage when it is combined with specific qualities on the remaining two temperament dimensions.

INVESTING BY THE SUBMISSIVE

External, and oftentimes chance, circumstances come into play in determining the investment objectives and strategies of submissive persons. Unlike dominant persons, submissive ones are more likely to have their goals set by others or by prevailing trends or fads in the investment world. Submissive persons usually do not act independently. They fail to study an investment area on their own, to selectively consult with knowledgeable others in the field, to summarize the information and principles they have learned, and to draw their own conclusions regarding appropriate investment actions. Instead, they are likely to seek guidance and advice from any source that at the time of action seems the most forceful or persuasive. These sources may be close friends, relatives, an author of a popular book, an investment salesperson or broker, an investment adviser, a banker, a charming stranger at a social gathering, a "spiritual" adviser, palm-reader, or fortune-teller, and last but not least, the mob.

If they invest in the faster paced stock or futures markets, submissive persons subscribe to investment newsletters and depend on one or more such sources for direction on what to do with their investments. Alternatively, they rely on the advice of brokers who handle their trades. In more extreme cases of submissiveness, such investors read several newsletters regularly and hold accounts at several brokerage houses, thinking that the more advice they get from different sources, the better off they are. Instead, the barrage of, usually contradictory, information from various sources simply adds to confusion and makes it difficult for these investors to stick to any particular investment plan.

Having committed to a particular investment, submissive individuals become dependent on the original source of advice for continued guidance and reassurance. If that source becomes unavailable or for some reason disappoints them, they cast around to find another person to advise and reassure them. The more difficulties they experience with an investment, the more desperately and frantically they cast aside advisers or confidants, replacing these with seemingly promising new ones. During such periods, they might follow the suggestions of anyone who is unusually confident and persuasive or who has the trappings of expertise.

Belief in luck is common among the submissive and helps explain some of their problems. By definition, a submissive individual is controlled and influenced more by others, external forces, and events, whereas a dominant one is more in charge of his actions and situations. This is why the submissive, compared with the dominant, lack confidence, self-assurance, and independence. A related characteristic is that the submissive, compared with the dominant, are more likely to believe in luck—to view various occurrences as being determined purely by chance and to be beyond their influence or control.

Belief in luck carries over to the ways in which the submissive regard events and changes associated with their investments. An overriding attitude is that they do not feel there is much they can do to influence the success or failure of their investments. It follows that they are less likely to study and prepare adequately to make investments. They rely on chance events or others' suggestions to make investment choices and, once they make an investment, fail to carry through with their plans because temporary reversals convince them easily that they have run out of luck and need to move on to other "luckier" situations.

There are two major ways, then, in which investments of submissive persons go wrong. The first is that, compared with dominant persons, they are more likely to become involved accidentally in an investment program of dubious merit. This can happen simply because they are impressed with the individual suggesting the program, irrespective of that person's level of technical know-how.

Second, submissive persons are less likely to adhere to an investment strategy after they have committed to it. Adherence to a realistically-based and carefully thought-out plan over a course of years and through transitory periods of adversity is a major ingredient of success in investing. Dominant persons are more apt to start with such a plan and then to adhere to it for lengthy periods. Submissive ones are less likely to begin with such a plan in the first place. If by some chance they do commit themselves to a sound plan and make the initiating transaction, they are less likely to follow it.

Since, compared with dominant persons, the submissive are less achievement-oriented, ambitious, competitive, risk-oriented, and confident, they typically select easier investment goals. In fact, because of their conservatism, they typically fail to take advantage of timely investment opportunities.

Generally, then, submissive individuals go along for long periods with their investment goals set too low. They overcome this meekness at the worst possible times when there is a strong popular conviction about the profitability of a particular type of investment. This is especially the case for those among the submissive who also are arousable.

MOB PSYCHOLOGY: A TRAP FOR THE SUBMISSIVE

A major investment pitfall for the submissive, especially when they also are arousable, is their tendency to be attracted to highly popular or fashionable investments. Lacking the necessary confidence to independently select their own investments, such persons often feel more secure when they observe others, particularly others in large numbers, making a certain investment choice.

This psychological force of the crowd or the mass has been discussed at length in the literature on investments. The common conviction and behavior of the crowd is irresistible for most of us and particularly for submissive and arousable individuals. Indeed, such persons may hesitate to participate when the crowd is thinner and when chances of success are greater. Instead, they wait until the crowd is considerably larger and its convictions are a roar. In this way, the magnetism of large numbers acting in conformity with one another draws in the submissive and commits them to investments at or near the very top of highly speculative markets.

INVESTMENT CYCLES AND THE SUBMISSIVE

Cyclical price swings in any investment medium are explained in terms of periods when the masses are disenchanted with a particular investment, be it real estate, gold, or the stock market, and when prices are very low. This is followed by initially slow and erratic price increases. Such price rises attract increasingly larger numbers to the particular type of investment, thus contributing to additional price increases. Price escalation accelerates because the number of participants increases geometrically as more and more are convinced it is an easy way to make money.

The majority of the investment public only becomes convinced of the value of an investment when prices are driven beyond reasonable and economically meaningful levels by large numbers of inexperienced speculators. Such a period of broad and speculative participation by the public usually culminates in frenzied and frothy markets where prices have little or no relationship to economic factors and where buyers are uninformed and inexperienced speculators acting as a crowd, or rather, like a mob.

When those who are caught up in the buying mania have used up not only their available cash but all their borrowing reserves to purchase all they can, the bulk of funds available for speculation is committed to the market. At this point, then, additional, substantial funds are lacking to sustain the upward momentum and this is when prices peak and begin to decline.

Once the decline begins, many are forced out or bail out because they were financially overextended and, having bought at or near the top, must sell to pay off loans. Their forced exit drives prices lower and exerts pressure on greater numbers to sell. The vicious cycle continues in this way until the majority of the public is disenchanted with the particular investment medium, most having sold with losses somewhere along the price decline.

The psychological pull of a rising market which increases demand and limits supply and the aversion to the subsequent declining market which increases supply and reduces demand are fundamental to analyses of cyclical up and down moves and the associated popularity levels of investment markets.

Of particular interest here is the lack of attraction for the submissive to investments which are at the trough or beginning stages of a cyclical up-move. It takes great daring, independence, and single mindedness (as with some dominant persons) to invest in something which most others shun and which generally is considered an easy way to lose money. This, indeed, is the reputation of investments which have reached their low point in a cycle.

On the other hand, when an investment becomes popular and the crowd surges to participate, the temptation to conform is great and is heightened especially for the submissive. Submissive persons find participation of the crowd reassuring and comforting and derive strength and courage from the conviction of many. They find it easier to take daring investment steps which they ordinarily would avoid when they are barraged with reports and claims of success and when they observe acquaint-

ances, friends, or relatives participating and actually suc-
ceeding.

Unfortunately, the crowd is the largest and the most
vociferous at the peak of a cycle and this is when the
submissive usually give up their reservations, stop hesitating, and take the plunge. In this way, they commit at
or near market tops and are soon exposed to rapid and
precipitous drops in the values of their investments.

JEFF: THE CASE OF A SUBMISSIVE INVESTOR

Jeff invested $100,000 in shares of a mutual fund close
to the stock market peak in the late sixties. Soon after,
the stock market began a long-term decline and he was
faced with varying, and usually high, paper losses over a
period of many years. There were times during this in-
terval when his mutual fund shares were worth as little
as $20,000.

Being timid, Jeff felt he could do nothing but wait.
Finally, in 1982, the value of his mutual fund shares
began to appreciate and by late 1982 had regained its lost
value. As his share values approached their original purchase price, Jeff could not wait to dispose of his investment. It is almost as if he had been trapped all those
years and now finally had a chance to escape the trap
and to "break even." Despite advice to the contrary, he
sold his shares at a 10 percent profit and watched in
dismay as their price continued to appreciate, doubling
in the following year.

This pattern of quiet suffering over an inordinately
long period followed by eagerness for release and escape
from an investment as soon as it begins to bear fruit is
common to some submissive persons. Holding on to an
investment in a total state of helplessness for a long
period accentuates their desire to escape it once they can
retrieve their capital.

As the investment begins to show a profit, and this only may be the beginning of a longer trend of gains, the accumulated anxiety and fear built up over the years create an exceedingly strong need to be rid of the investment. As a consequence, the submissive investor sells prematurely and with a small gain to rid herself of all the negative feelings the investment generates and simply to forget the painful experience. In her mind, she at least has come out better than even and this justifies the sale. But, considering inflation, the minimal returns during the holding period, and the psychological costs, it is a huge loss. More importantly, the premature sale forestalls benefits from a long-term cyclical up-move which could make the investment worthwhile.

Chapter 7
A Complete Description of Temperament

Each of the three basic dimensions of temperament (pleasantness, arousability, dominance) provides valuable information to describe and understand an individual and her investment style. These three dimensions are foundation blocks for a description of temperament. Being independent of one another, each provides unique and distinctive information about a person. Thus, if we know one of these characteristics of a person, it tells us nothing about the other two—each quality provides information that is separate and unrelated to that obtained from the remaining two. Together, the three dimensions are both necessary and sufficient for a comprehensive description of temperament.

The temperament of a given person, then, is defined completely when we can assign a specific value to her on each of the pleasant-unpleasant, arousable-unarousable, and dominant-submissive dimensions. It is the unique combination of these three values which is most useful for understanding that individual and for analyzing her investment style with the objective of improving her investment performance.

One way to use the three dimensions and develop a taxonomy to describe each individual is to dichotomize each of the dimensions (e.g., pleasant versus unpleasant, dominant versus submissive). These rough subdivisions yield the following eight combinations which constitute the eight basic temperament types.

Exuberant = pleasant, arousable, dominant
Dependent = pleasant, arousable, submissive
Relaxed = pleasant, unarousable, dominant
Docile = pleasant, unarousable, submissive
Hostile = unpleasant, arousable, dominant
Anxious = unpleasant, arousable, submissive
Disdainful = unpleasant, unarousable, dominant
Bored = unpleasant, unarousable, submissive

The following brief characterizations of each of the eight temperament types and some of their interrelationships are helpful as an overview of subsequent chapters in which each is described in greater detail.

THE EXUBERANT TEMPERAMENT

"Exuberant" (pleasant, arousable, dominant) persons have positive social expectations, thus, being outgoing, friendly, and extroverted, and are able to take charge of situations. They favor varied, stimulating, sensuous, fun, playful, and impulsive activities. The exuberant also like to take chances or even dangerous risks, help others, make suggestions, or become the center of attention.

You can have positive social expectations and be friendly in a quiet or restrained way and this happens when someone has a pleasant and unarousable temperament. In contrast, the exuberant have social and work-related activities that are more expressive, excitement-laden, highly active, unrestrained, and risky.

For the exuberant, investments tend to become playthings rather than matters of serious consideration. They approach investments impulsively, without much thoughtful preparation. Their attitudes to investments are reminiscent of the gambler's who seeks high risk and fast pace for excitement and fun. As a consequence, the exuberant do not make good investors and need constant reminders to stay away from high-uncertainty investments.

THE BORED TEMPERAMENT

The exact opposite of exuberant is "bored" (unpleasant, unarousable, submissive). The bored are melancholic, brooding, and gloomy. They are socially withdrawn and spend much time alone, engaged in solitary activities. They have a low level of energy, often feel tired, sleep long hours without feeling refreshed, and feel helpless or impotent to deal with their life situations and problems.

In extreme cases, the bored become hypochondriacal and are preoccupied with one or more imaginary physical ailments. They spend many hours in bed or sleeping during the day because they do not have the energy or positive outlook to initiate a social activity, do something physical like a sport, or work. They become inattentive to physical appearance, seeming unkempt and unattractive or even bizarre because of failure to wash, attend to hair or makeup, or clean clothing.

In these extreme cases of boredom, there is an inertia associated with low-arousal states. It is difficult for the bored to make transitions to high-arousal activities such as going out with a group of friends or even calling a friend on the phone, doing some housecleaning, going out for a walk, let alone taking on more work or a new investment. All of these activities require an increase in arousal in the form of greater physical activity and mental alertness and the change feels too discontinuous and burdensome—it is much easier to go on in a low-arousal state.

Although the investment activities of those who are moderately versus highly exuberant differ only in terms of quantitative changes, with more extreme exuberants simply doing more of what moderate ones do, this is not the case with the bored. Moderately bored persons are tempted greatly by persons, situations, or investments which do not appear to require much effort and that can induce feelings of elation, excitement, and happiness. Thus, the apparent and deceptive "magical" or easy relief from boredom that high-uncertainty investments provide constitutes a clear danger to the moderately bored.

In this way, the moderately bored are highly attracted to exuberant persons; exciting situations, particularly those where they can be passive, such as high-paced games or movies; stimulant drugs, food, and alcohol; or high-uncertainty investments. Their participation is not active and constructive, but rather a passive involvement. Often they do not even have energy to seek out and get involved with such persons and situations, but when the opportunity comes along, they find it very appealing.

In contrast, extremely bored individuals feel thoroughly helpless and hopeless, lacking motivation for the most elementary means of improving their personal, social, or financial circumstances. In the realm of investments, then, such persons are apt to have a defeatist attitude associated with extreme inactivity or lack of participation.

THE DEPENDENT TEMPERAMENT

"Dependent" (pleasant, arousable, submissive) persons are like exuberant ones in their positive social expectations and their enjoyment of, and attachment to, friends and social situations. But, they differ from the exuberant in that the dependent are submissive. Thus, in social groups, exuberant members take charge and guide others while dependent ones go along with the wishes and plans of other group members. Exuberant individuals take chances, form independent opinions, or initiate projects;

dependent ones tend to be more conservative, entering situations only after others have led the way, joining projects or activities organized by others, and adhering to the attitudes, values, opinions, and life-styles of those whom they like and respect.

Dependent persons especially need, and turn to, others in time of difficulty, as when they have to learn something new, or have interpersonal problems, job-related anxieties, failures, mishaps, pains, or illnesses. They often try to have others extricate them from their problems by taking care of everything. They usually turn to others for advice and direction, cannot seem to follow these on their own, and return over and over again for further assistance. Frequently, they are disappointed or upset when they cannot get more attention, assistance, or more effective suggestions.

Many of the negative associations we have to dependency result from the clinging and excessively demanding characteristics of the dependent. They do not seem to have sufficient initiative to carry through with a project once others help them get started and require continued support, encouragement, and direction.

Of all the temperament types, the dependent are the most conforming to social and group pressures. They are likely to wholeheartedly and unquestioningly espouse a package of ideas and life-style promulgated by some offbeat group or some authority figure.

In the area of investments, the dependent get most of their ideas from people they know and like rather than from objective sources such as books or learned articles on a particular investment topic. Therefore, they lack the sense of confidence which comes with extensive independent study and the careful balancing of various factors which go into planning one's own investments.

Whatever confidence they have in their selected approach to investments is acquired through contagion from the individual who gave them the idea in the first place. This confidence is shattered easily when they see that individual changing investment tactics, experiencing difficulties with his own investments, or expressing doubts about the approach.

THE DISDAINFUL TEMPERAMENT

The exact opposite of dependent is "disdainful" (unpleasant, unarousable, dominant). The disdainful have negative social expectations, meaning that they do not find social relationships enjoyable, gratifying, or helpful and instead find them boring, unsatisfying, and troublesome.

Disdainful persons do not usually establish warm or loving relationships, tending to keep to themselves socially and at work, and getting involved with others when such involvement is necessitated by their plans or is to their benefit.

The disdainful are contemptuous, aloof, and uncaring. They are uninterested in the affairs of others and are not moved easily by the happiness or grief of the people they know.

Just as they are callous about others, they can be highly self-disciplined about themselves, able to delay gratification, and to drive hard and endlessly to achieve their goals. In work or investments, they are likely to be contemptuous of others, viewing others as competitors or obstacles. They are likely to derive pleasure from seeing others do poorly, especially when a comparison with their own performance is meaningful and flattering to themselves. Indeed, as the disdainful strive to achieve their own goals, they are not likely to be bothered when others get hurt in the process. In fact, disdainful persons abound among the ranks of the "professional," as distinct from the impulsive and violent, criminal.

The disdainful are defensive, mistrustful, and suspicious. They are quick to unduly and inappropriately infer negative insinuations, insult, rejection, or deliberate and calculated harmful intentions on the part of others. But, unlike "hostile" persons, they do not respond openly, impulsively, or violently to such inferred negative thrusts; rather, they withdraw and carefully and calmly plan a strategy to redress the balance.

Generally, disdainful persons approach emotionally difficult situations calmly and with deliberation. They feel dominant and self-confident, knowing they can act independently and successfully in problem situations. Further, their low arousability permits them to maintain detachment and, thereby, to gain a broad perspective and deal successfully with complex and changing situations which would overwhelm the arousable.

Disdainful persons have very good chances of success with their investments and can do well even when investments involve high levels of uncertainty. Calm detachment is a definite asset in competition and in the highly emotional circumstances associated with investments. Disdainful persons benefit greatly from their ability to remove themselves physically and psychologically from emotionally volatile situations and, thereby, to rationally consider their various options. They are likely to view the arena of investments as a sort of competition with numerous incompetent opponents—their gains being others' losses. Success at investments is highly reinforcing to them because it reconfirms their sense of self-worth and superiority.

THE RELAXED TEMPERAMENT

The "relaxed" (pleasant, unarousable, dominant) temperament is psychologically the healthiest. This temperament provides natural immunity to stress which generates feelings of displeasure, arousal, and submissiveness. Of course, relaxed persons also experience discomfort, irritation, and anxiety in stressful situations. But, for a given level of stress, they experience less anxiety than others who possess different temperament characteristics.

The relaxed have positive social expectations and value friendships and close relationships, but differ from the exuberant in that they are less active and emotional in how they socialize. Also, compared with the exuberant, they are less involved with people, not needing social contacts as much, and being able to assume more detached and appraising attitudes toward relationships.

Being dominant, the relaxed place great emphasis (even more than the exuberant) on control of their personal activities, work, plans, and surroundings. Compared with the exuberant, they strive less for dominance in casual and fun social situations. Relaxed persons, more than the exuberant, are apt to emphasize excellence in their careers and to strive for high goals in the various hobbies, sports, or financial activities they undertake. In terms of their determination to achieve goals, the relaxed are very much like the disdainful.

In investing, the relaxed tend to plan carefully and independently. They personally develop and initiate a plan, are deliberate and cautious instead of impulsive, and are able to maintain a proper perspective on their strategy despite temporary difficulties or setbacks. Relaxed persons have the most advantageous temperament for investment success because of their resilience to stress and their manner of approach to life problems already noted.

THE ANXIOUS TEMPERAMENT

The exact opposite of relaxed is "anxious" (unpleasant, arousable, submissive). The anxious temperament is the least healthy psychologically. Characteristics of this temperament consistently aggravate the effects of stress, difficulties, and problems which in themselves are associated with feelings of displeasure, arousal, and submissiveness. Indeed, the extremely anxious are generally referred to as "neurotic"—thus, "neuroticism" is simply another label for a highly anxious temperament.

Anxious individuals have been the most prominent in classical analyses of psychological disturbance and dysfunction. In contrast, *within our system of description, the common denominator of all forms of psychopathology is an unpleasant temperament.* Unpleasant temperament includes negative social expectations and more general negative expectations (pessimism) about life that result in unsatisfying social relationships, social isolation, and unhappiness. When unpleasantness is extreme, the individual is defensive, tends to be suspicious regarding the intentions of others, and sometimes is even paranoid.

Combinations of extreme unpleasantness with extremes on the remaining two dimensions of temperament yield four basic types of psychopathology: bored, disdainful, anxious, and hostile.

Boredom and anxiety are two distinct clinical syndromes. Disdainful and hostile characteristics are "character disorders" in traditional psychiatric terminology. The latter two help describe anti-social and sociopathic individuals, such as criminals or persons on the criminal fringe who exploit others to their own advantage without regard to cost or harm to people and institutions. The difference between the disdainful and hostile is that the former are more "professional," calculating, deliberate, and nonviolent in their criminal activities, whereas the latter are more volatile, impulsive, highly aggressive, and physically violent.

Our general description of psychopathology helps place "normal" and "abnormal" temperament in proper perspective. Remembering that each temperament dimension is a continuum, it is important to note that each of these dimensions characterizes a great variety of normal individuals and only is useful for describing psychopathology for those who occupy the most extreme ranges of these continua.

When we refer to someone as "anxious" this does not mean necessarily that the person is psychologically disturbed or neurotic. Instead, it describes a set of emotional predispositions that occur commonly in the general population. Only when the three temperament qualities of anxiety take on extreme values does reference to psychopathology become relevant and meaningful. In this volume, we deal primarily with the normal range of variations in temperament characteristics and the implications of these for investments.

Specifically, anxious individuals tend to have lives often complicated by worries, unresolved difficulties and problems, insecurity, unhappiness, and dissatisfaction; conflicts with others and feelings of being hurt and abused by others; accidents, mishaps, failures, forgetfulness, and insomnia; and dependency on drugs which have relaxing or tranquilizing effects.

In the same difficult situations and, in comparison with the relaxed, anxious persons are more likely to fret, worry, be unhappy, complain, feel uneasy, upset, and dissatisfied, and to have difficulty coping. Coping problems are likely to arise due to frequent errors, mistakes, and accidents, inability to concentrate and maintain perspective on all relevant aspects of a situation, distraction by disturbing aspects of a situation which may be irrelevant to the task at hand, and inability to deal planfully and independently with a situation.

Negative feelings of discomfort, irritation, frustration, concern, anxiety, or fear induced by one difficult situation last longer for the anxious than for the relaxed and are more likely to spill over into other situations or encounters with people.

Generally, situations that are high in uncertainty are highly arousing for the people in them. When high uncertainty and its arousing effect are combined with pleasantness, the result is excitement and elation; in contrast, when high uncertainty is combined with unpleasantness, the result is stress. In the case of high-uncertainty investments, the difficulties, setbacks, and frequent financial drain more often generate unpleasant rather than pleasant feelings. This is why the level of uncertainty of investments is proportional to the amount of discomfort, distress, problems, and anxieties for investors.

For anxious persons, these effects of high uncertainty are felt the most. Even small difficulties with an investment are likely to be blown out of proportion and to become a psychological drain for the anxious. This is why anxious individuals do poorly at high-uncertainty, and even moderate-uncertainty, investments.

Since investments often require tolerance of periods of adversity and adherence to a reasoned game plan to achieve success, low tolerance of difficult periods (usually due to interference from emotional reactions) means greater chances of failure. Anxious persons find such temporary setbacks psychologically intolerable and bail out at any cost just to relieve themselves of worry, sleeplessness, misery, or even terror. The need to bail out is strongest when an investment is doing poorly—is worth less. As a consequence, the sale of an investment at such a juncture leads to losses while giving the investor relief from pain and anxiety.

Anxious investors are therefore best off with stable, unchanging, and low-risk investments which generate positive cash flow. If they get involved with moderate-uncertainty investments, their chances of success are enhanced when professionals manage their investments so they do not have to deal with intricate details, decisions, and problems of the investments on a day-to-day basis.

THE DOCILE TEMPERAMENT

"Docile" (pleasant, unarousable, submissive) persons resemble the dependent, differing from the latter because they are less arousable. Although docile individuals have positive social expectations and value friendships and close relationships, they generally are less involved with, or needy of, social contacts than pleasant and arousable (e.g., dependent, exuberant) persons. Compared with the dependent, docile persons are less likely to seek assistance and guidance from others. Also, they are more tolerant of discomfort, pain, or difficulties encountered at work or at home because they do not feel as anxious.

The docile are less emotional and more placid compared with the dependent. When confronted with interpersonal problems, job-related difficulties, mishaps, accidents, setbacks, or illnesses, docile, compared with dependent, persons' search for assistance is less desperate and frantic and more sensible and objective. As a consequence, they have more success in obtaining reliable information, competent advice or help, and in coping with the many difficulties we all encounter daily.

Docile persons, thus, manifest many strengths of the relaxed and only differ from the latter in that they are submissive. Like relaxed persons, they are calm and level-headed in difficult situations. But, compared with relaxed persons, they are more likely to seek guidance from others to help initiate and carry out their plans.

Among the four submissive temperament types (dependent, docile, anxious, bored), the docile are best equipped temperamentally to search for, carefully study and evaluate, and then select competent sources to manage their investments. Also, once having made such a choice, they are likely to stay with it and the selected program of investments despite market reversals and adversities.

When they invest for themselves, docile persons encounter some of the difficulties we noted for submissive individuals in general. Since their investment choices and plans often are externally determined, they lack confidence in their plans. Like all submissive persons, they doubt their particular investment strategies, decisions, or actions during periods when their investments do poorly. However, compared with the other three submissive types, they are less fickle or capricious and are less likely to change investment strategies mid-course.

THE HOSTILE TEMPERAMENT

The exact opposite of docile is "hostile" (unpleasant, arousable, dominant). The hostile can be described as rigid, inflexible, aggressive, or authoritarian. Narcissists also are typically hostile or disdainful. Psychoanalysts used the concept "obsessive-compulsive" to refer to somewhat extreme and pathological variants of hostile temperament. The most extreme pathological form is "paranoid schizophrenia" where suspicion, mistrust, secretiveness, and fear of harm from others alternate with aggressive and angry over-reactions because of overly exaggerated inferences of the negativism and malice of others.

Like the anxious, hostile persons are emotional in negative ways, being easily upset or rattled. However, where the anxious submit to pain and suffer internally, the hostile attribute their pain and difficulties to outside sources and agents and are likely to attack, hurt, damage, or even destroy those sources. They also often insist on imposing their attitudes and values on others. Having people submit to them in this way is soothing.

The unpleasant component of a hostile temperament implies negative social expectations. Like the disdainful, hostile persons have difficulty forming warm or loving relationships, although they are more needy of such relationships than the disdainful. Like disdainful persons, hostile ones are quick to infer negative insinuation, rejection, or insult. They tend to be mistrustful and suspicious of others. The close relationships they develop involve secretiveness, suspicion, excessive disagreement, altercations, rejections, violent conflicts, separations, and periods of quiet rage or hatred.

More than any other temperament type, the hostile often are bothered, irritated, critical, disgusted, and angered. A minor driving mishap, an erroneous billing, an unduly lengthy wait in a line or at a stop light, a letter of rejection, a low evaluation by superiors, or poor performance of investments can arouse these feelings. This leads to a desire, or actions designed, to hurt the inferred source of pain. Anger is manifested as irritability, seething inner rage without expression but evidenced as tension and withdrawal, sarcasm or put-downs, criticisms, verbal tirades, or various degrees of violent physical action.

Whereas a disdainful person would plan carefully to gain the upper hand in a conflict with others, a hostile one is likely to blurt out his disenchantment or complaints or to lash out impulsively and violently.

The hostile do very poorly at investing. The only temperament category to do worse is the anxious. Hostile individuals are emotional and impulsive in making an investment choice and in committing money to it. Unlike unarousable and dominant persons, they are less likely to research and study the field in which they invest.

Initial poor planning reduces chances of success by increasing probabilities of setbacks mid-stream. Also, hostile individuals are likely to react with extreme anger when investments do not do well. Because of this anger, they typically make mistakes which either maximize losses or minimize gains.

Remember that anger tends to narrow one's perspective, making it difficult to judge a complex investment situation in a balanced way. So, when an investment shows a temporary setback while still having a good chance of long-term success, the hostile are prone to overlook the long-term potential. In such circumstances, the hostile sell prematurely because of anger with themselves, their investment, or their broker — the sale simply helps vent the anger and expresses rejection and disgust at something which is painful.

COMBINATIONS

Knowing the preceding eight types of temperament helps us understand someone who is extreme on two temperament dimensions but neutral on the third. Supposing, for instance, Oliver is pleasant and submissive, but neutral on arousability. He, thus, is a cross between the dependent and docile and we can formulate his temperament by averaging the characteristics of the latter two.

Those of you who are analytically inclined will appreciate the following straightforward approach to combinations. Let us use shorthand notations as follows:

+P = Pleasant	–P = Unpleasant
+A = Arousable	–A = Unarousable
+D = Dominant	–D = Submissive

One interpretation of saying Oliver represents an equal combination of dependent (+P+A–D) and docile (+P–A–D) is that he acts dependent half the time and docile the other half. In terms of our shorthand notation, Oliver's temperament is computed as follows:

$$0.5 \times (+P+A-D) + 0.5 \times (+P-A-D) = +P-D$$

So, as already noted, all we need to know about Oliver is that he has a pleasant and submissive temperament.

Very few people are exactly neutral on any temperament dimension. Most lean more toward one end than the other. Even though almost neutral, Oliver may lean more toward being arousable (or unarousable). If this were to be the case, we would form a mental average of dependent and docile characteristics for Oliver, emphasizing dependent attributes if he tends toward arousability and weight docile qualities more if he tends toward low arousability.

Sometimes, a person is neutral on two temperament dimensions and only extreme on the third. For instance, if someone is extreme only on arousability, then that individual's characteristics and investment style are inferred readily by reviewing our chapter on arousable-unarousable persons.

One reader of this volume told me she thought she was an equal combination of the relaxed (+P − A + D) and dependent (+ P + A − D) temperaments. She wanted to know how I would describe that combination. The answer, simply, is as follows:

$$0.5 \times (+P - A + D) + 0.5 \times (+P + A - D) = +P$$

The single resulting value of +P shows she has a pleasant temperament. To understand her temperament characteristics and her instinctive investment approach, she would only need to study our basic chapter on pleasant-unpleasant temperament (Chapter 4).

COMBINATIONS OF LIFE CIRCUMSTANCES AND TEMPERAMENT

An important advantage of the preceding eight categories of temperament is that we can use a straightforward translation to explain the emotional impact of life circumstances.

An exuberant person may work at a job which is peaceful, harmonious, and rewarding or one which is hectic and stressful. Someone who is dependent may have a supportive and caring mate or one who is rejecting and hostile. Any of these persons may go through a multi-year economic recession where incomes are drastically reduced and financial hardships are magnified. Alternatively, any one of them may come into a large inheritance or win a large sum in a lottery.

All conditions and changes associated with work, home life, or extended family constitute life circumstances and, in addition to temperament, contribute to how we feel and influence how we invest. The framework we have outlined here is helpful for analyzing the emotional impact of life circumstances. Before considering the latter, however, we need first to examine each of the eight temperament types in greater detail.

Chapter 8
The Exuberant

Steve works in public relations. In college, when he was considering career alternatives, friends often told him he would be good at public relations because of his innate ability to get along with people. He was an average student because he spent more time socializing with his fraternity friends and playing basketball than studying. Even when he was back at the fraternity house and at his desk ready to work, he was interrupted frequently by telephone calls from friends outside the house. Public relations did not require highly technical preparation and seemed to provide a balance between his modest scholastic achievements and his superior social abilities, so that was the direction he took.

After graduation, he applied to several firms and the very first one to interview him offered him a job. His interviewer liked him, his easy manner, his sense of humor, his ability to be spontaneous and open in both the way he answered questions about himself and the way in which he showed interest and curiosity in the job. Now, after five years with the same firm, he continues to be well-liked by his peers as well as by senior partners. He and his wife enjoy giving parties for firm members and they are almost invariably invited when others organize a social gathering.

Steve has been very successful at his work. Despite his junior standing, he has managed to bring in several large accounts involving some of his old college friends or their contacts.

A couple of years ago, Steve decided to invest some of his extra income in the stock market. Ever since, he has been a steady and active trader. Unfortunately, despite the considerable effort he has put into the market, keeping up with his investments, and making trading decisions, he has had little profit to show for it.

His problem is his enthusiasm and desire for a fast pace of activity. He hears about a company, talks to his broker about it, checks it out himself, and decides that it is a worthwhile investment. He buys the stock believing he has a very good chance of making 50 percent or more within a year. If he happens to be right and the stock moves up soon after the purchase and then stalls for a while or pulls back slightly, he sells even when his profit is only 10 to 15 percent. At that point, his thoughts are that if he can make 10 or 15 percent within a month, he might as well take his profits and go on to something else that is about to make a sudden up move.

He also does not hesitate to sell when a stock moves against him; he'd rather take a 10 percent loss than hold on and hope the stock will recover. Here, his rationale is that if the stock is acting weak, there must be some negative factors that are not known publicly and which did not enter his calculations prior to purchase. Anyway, he hates to hold on to dogs—he'd rather get rid of them and move on to bigger and better things.

Steve's stock trading strategy is molded by his adventurism and enthusiasm. There are always many more stocks that he would like to own than he has money for. He gets excited about the prospects of different companies for a variety of reasons: better earnings, a new and successful product, an anticipated buy-out, recent accumulation of shares by a large holder, an increase in dividend, or a stock split. Usually, the rosy scenario he forecasts includes imminent changes.

He hates not being in the fray and having to watch from the sidelines by virtue of not owning a stock. Indeed, some of his expectations are confirmed and, it seems, particularly when he has not yet had a chance to buy a stock. The way this works is that when you are enthusiastic about thirty or forty companies, there are bound to be positive developments for one or two of them each month.

When he in fact buys a stock, subjectively, for him, the pace of action slows considerably. Usually, there are no surprises or large price moves and he quickly loses interest. The fascination with, and attraction of, the unknown—the stocks he does not yet own—far outweigh the interest generated by the known—the stock he has bought. He spends more time thinking about stocks he does not own than the ones he holds in his portfolio. This explains his willingness to sell at a small profit even when he is right, because there are so many other situations which he feels are superior and where he is bound to make more money quickly.

If it weren't for his many well-placed contacts that often provide him with valuable information about stock market opportunities, his active trading pace would probably result in steady losses. As it is, Steve manages to eke out a profit no greater than what he could earn easily by leaving the funds in a savings account. But he continues to be optimistic and to feel that he'll make it big in the market one of these days.

Steve's temperament is at the core of his investment problem. Being exuberant, he likes to be spontaneous, active, adventuresome, in charge, and to have fun. This also means that instead of planning for the long range, he would rather be impulsive and make investment decisions on the spur of the moment. To him, it is like a sporting event. When his side loses (or his company does not do well), it isn't a catastrophe—he can bail out easily and quickly. On the other hand, he can have lots of fun if his impulsive and easy decision is a correct one and he makes a nice chunk of money on his investment in a short time.

Steve's generally positive outlook and confidence make it possible for him to jump in and out of stocks in ways which many others would avoid because of anxiety or fear. Unfortunately, his fearlessness goes hand in hand with a lack of a deliberate, long-term strategy which requires patience and discipline. Steve is a short-term trader, not a long-term investor. Frequent trading within the course of a week or even a month is costly because trading gains must offset accumulating commission costs. Very few private investors succeed as short-term investors because of this commission handicap and because short-term jagged price moves in stock or futures markets are extremely difficult to anticipate. Steve, however, is not humbled by these complexities and unfavorable odds. For him, the market is a challenge which he feels he can take on in his typical cavalier manner.

You may recall Jennifer from the "Cases" chapter. She seemed always to be involved in the hottest and most talked about investments of the day. She loved to be the center of attention, to discuss her investments, give the impression of expertise, authority, and control, and to emphasize her more successful exploits. Jennifer who was also exuberant tended to use her investments more like a hobby, dabbling in these with small sums of money. Unlike Steve, Jennifer seemed less interested in the financial goals of investing and did not mind the steady small losses because of the more important social benefits she gained from these activities.

THE GAMBLER'S SYNDROME

In many ways, Steve and Jennifer's emotional attitudes toward investments resemble that of gamblers. Typically, gamblers are motivated by the thrill of the activity, excitement of selecting bets, fast pace of action, contagious elation of the crowd, drama, social benefits and stimulation, special roles or identities assumed during gambling, and exaggerated and unrealistic hopes. It is not surprising that institutions which cater to gamblers provide a large number of perquisites to facilitate these incidental emotional benefits: expensively and sometimes outlandishly decorated hotels, complimentary rooms or meals, lavish entertainment, all designed to enhance feelings of a distinctive, activity-packed, high-status, exuberant experience.

Like Steve and many exuberant types, gamblers enjoy the activity, bustle, and atmosphere more than the results. It is the *process*, the means, rather than the end result which provides the essential emotional reinforcers. Indeed, the end result takes on less significance in that usually it entails losses.

Among the various temperament types we consider, the exuberant and the bored are the most prone to approach investments with a gambler's mental and emotional attitudes. In this sense, they are the most likely to become "addicted" investors. For them, the process of investing takes on an unduly large emotional significance. Fast and active pace are essential, investment rationale is lacking, the style tends to be impatient, fun-oriented, and undisciplined, and losses can get out of hand.

Exuberant persons assume this investment approach because it is consistent with their general pattern of behavior. Bored individuals invest in this way to *escape* boredom. Like a stimulant drug, this style of investing provides temporary relief from boredom, despair, and hopelessness. It is an antidote to boredom because it generates feelings of pleasure, arousal, and dominance. Since gambling, and a gambler's approach to investments, provides much needed emotional relief to the bored, it follows that they, more than the exuberant, are likely to become addicted compulsively to these activities.

Steve does not have an addictive investment style, but he, nevertheless, has a problem. He devotes a lot of time and effort to an activity outside his profession and shows little benefit for all his work. Perhaps the investing also detracts from his ability to be even more successful at work.

WRITING DOWN ONE'S TRADING RULES

Given our explanation of Steve's investment style in terms of his temperament, what can he do to improve his income from investments? He has several options. One of these is to write down a few stock trading rules for himself and adhere to these as closely as possible.

Writing out a carefully thought out investment strategy is valuable because the simple act of organizing one's thoughts on paper gives them more weight in the struggle against impulsive and emotional behavior. First of all, if Steve were to write down an unbiased summary of his current strategy, he would recognize its futility—an endless series of counterbalancing small profits and losses. He would be forced to modify his trading pattern to include longer-term holding of profitable choices so as to have large profits offsetting small losses.

One set of new rules for Steve might be as follows: (1) sell a stock if its price declines 10 percent below the purchase price, and (2) if a stock appreciates after its purchase, hold it as long as it does not drop more than 10 percent below its most recent peak. These are two elementary trading rules (and, of course, there are other far more sophisticated ones he might follow).

The rules would be written out clearly and he would try to follow them to the letter. There is no guarantee he would follow the rules, but having made the decision to do so, Steve would have instituted substantial safeguards against his emotional tendency to seek activity for activity's sake, to seek stimulation, and to be playful or impulsive.

Any strategy we might recommend to Steve would have to counteract his hyper or almost manic trading activity, force him to slow down, plan a reasoned strategy, and then attempt to follow it. The first option of writing down rules is, thus, appropriate, but requires considerable self-discipline. Being dominant, Steve has an edge in this department.

SELECTING A SLOW-PACED MEDIUM

A second approach which does not require as much discipline is for Steve to try an investment medium where it is difficult to execute purchases or sales. Real estate is one such medium. If Steve were to concentrate on real estate investments, he would be forced to spend more time considering the pros and cons of a purchase because such a purchase is usually involved, time consuming, and requires enforced waiting periods. These delays and complexities, plus the substantial broker commissions in real estate transactions, make it harder for investors to be active traders. The sizeable commissions in themselves necessitate longer holding periods—there has to be enough appreciation to at least pay the commission. It also takes several months to sell a property once a decision has been made to do so. All in all, the slower pace of real estate transactions tends to force a more deliberate, calculated, and cautious attitude, and thereby would counteract Steve's temperament-based inclinations.

A related alternative is for Steve to go in on a partnership with a few friends to purchase real estate. His job would be to manage the day-to-day affairs of the partnership while other, more savvy partners would have the final say on what and when to buy and when to sell. The advantage of this arrangement is that it would use Steve's strengths in dealing with people—his partners as well as those leasing the property. More importantly, it would keep Steve highly active and give him a sense of control on a daily basis. He could put his skills to use soliciting new lessees, ensure that the property is properly maintained, and that new or renewed leases are negotiated advantageously. All this would reduce his need to have purchases and sales become the focus of activity.

USING INVESTMENT MANAGERS

Another approach involves the use of money managers. We know Steve likes to be in charge, so we won't suggest that he place all his saving in the care of one. Instead, he might begin by placing only 1/3 to 1/2 of his savings in a mutual fund or have them managed by a professional who invests directly for individual clients.

After a year's trial period, Steve would have a chance to check his own performance against that of the managed funds. Based on this comparison, he could decide to increase or decrease the percentage of funds that is managed professionally. This step-wise strategy could work because effortlessly and painlessly obtained higher returns from managed funds would be a very strong inducement to relinquish control, at least in this one sphere of his life. Anyway, he could use the comfortably earned extra income to generate adventure and excitement in nonfinancial areas of his life.

TYPICAL INVESTMENT STYLE OF THE EXUBERANT

A general analysis of ways in which exuberant persons approach their investments, the problems they encounter, and ways to improve their investment strategies must be based on the specific characteristics of this temperament and the emotional effects of investments.

Being pleasant, arousable, and dominant, exuberant individuals approach investments in the same ways they approach other activities: they are optimistic; sensuous, fun-oriented, playful, and impulsive; socially gregarious, inclined to take charge, be the center of attention, or even tend toward exhibitionism; and, thus, enjoy varied stimulation from changing, unpredictable, and possibly risky activities.

It follows that in investing they tend to be unduly optimistic; select high-uncertainty (complex, varied, rapidly changing, unpredictable, novel) investments; are casual, fun-oriented, playful, and sometimes impulsive instead of cautious, deliberate, patient, steady, and planful; and use investments to provide material for more interesting and varied social contacts and conversations or as a basis for exhibitionistic displays in social situations.

All of these emotional inclinations are counterproductive to investment success. Undue optimism is unrealistic in investing, particularly when high uncertainty is involved. Indeed, high-uncertainty investments often have problems and disappointing reverses. The exuberant, being arousable, is wont to become emotionally enmeshed in the short-term adversities instead of taking the longer-term view.

High-uncertainty investments typically generate high arousal in combination with more displeasure than pleasure. The combination of exuberant temperament (pleasant, arousable, dominant) with the emotional impact of such investments (displeasure, high arousal) results in neutral pleasure or even displeasure, very high arousal, and dominance (i.e., irritation, disgust, or anger).

An angry investor is likely to behave rashly and impulsively, taking steps which are influenced mostly by immediate and short-term considerations and which are not moderated by the longer-term investment strategy. For instance, the investor may sell a property, a stock, or a commodity in anger, figuratively "striking out against the misbehaving investment" and regret the action a day or two later while rethinking the circumstances in a calmer mood.

Playful, fun-oriented, adventuresome, and impulsive attitudes toward investments are harmful because chances of success are much greater with deliberate planning and steady and steadfast adherence to a long-term strategy. Long-term strategy and perspective help one overcome short-term adversities by reminding oneself of the overall profit balance after the short-term swings are averaged.

Using investments to spice up social exchanges or to show off socially tends to introduce a variety of irrelevant and often unproductive mental commitments regarding one's investments. For example, someone who brags to her friends about how well her investments are doing will believe her own social playacting and become overly confident or greedy and, thereby, miss a good opportunity to sell at a nice profit or miss tell-tale signs of impending negative developments.

The implications of all this for the exuberant are that it is important to rein in enthusiasm and risk orientation by selecting investments that are lower in uncertainty than those which instinctively and unthinkingly would seem more appealing. Lower-uncertainty investments managed by oneself or slightly higher-uncertainty ones managed by experts may seem dull, slow-paced, and uninteresting. But, this is exactly the cure against treating investments as objects of fun and play, or as vehicles of social conversation and exhibitionism.

FAST-PACED MARKETS — TRAPS FOR THE EXUBERANT

Also, exuberant persons need to be watchful especially during unusual, fast-paced market conditions. Let us take the stock market to illustrate this point. More often than not the broad market moves slowly and gradually, and is generally dull. But, on occasion the volume of transactions escalates suddenly and prices of many issues move up or down dramatically. Similarly, for lengthy periods, most individual issues have small and insignificant fluctuations in value with moderate transaction volumes, but for some isolated periods of a few days to a few weeks an issue may have dramatic up or down moves on very high volume.

Whether it is the entire market or a particular issue, large movements and high volumes are conducive to high arousal states. When price changes are rapid and favorable, pleasure and high arousal from the events combine with an exuberant temperament to generate high excitement and a desire for a highly active, fun-like pace. Under these circumstances, the exuberant trade much too frequently, thus, minimizing gains due to large commission and execution (bid versus ask) costs. When price changes are rapid and unfavorable, displeasure and high arousal created by the market combine with an exuberant temperament to generate very high degrees of irritation, disgust, or anger. In such instances, exuberant types act rashly and impulsively, tending to forget their longer-term strategies.

In short, fast-paced markets increase the emotional vulnerability of exuberant persons. Someone with this temperament may be able to overcome his emotional handicaps when markets are changing slowly and gradually, but lose his self control in a high-paced market. Thus, exuberant persons need to diffuse the emotional impact of such markets by deliberately reducing their proximity to, or involvement with, them. They need to force themselves to turn to other activities and away from investments and to think about their investments at a distance with more detached attitudes. High-paced markets should automatically ring warning bells!

Generally, exuberant persons need to rein in their optimism and need for excitement, variety, risk, and fun in their investment efforts. Being aware of their emotional inclinations and how these place them at a disadvantage in handling moderate to high-uncertainty investments is a most important initial step. More cautious planning and greater commitment to a well-planned strategy with lower-uncertainty investments is the second step.

If the exuberant feel that they might be giving up something by undertaking this more cautious and less exciting approach, they only need remember the aggravation and anger generated by past failures. They also might consider the many fun ways in which they can spend the small but steady investment income that can be obtained from low-uncertainty investments without stress.

Chapter 9

The Dependent

Jackie is an attorney. Her father was a builder and her brother has followed in the same line of business. She is single and has retained close ties with both her mother and her brother. Jackie is sociable and would much rather be with people than alone. She definitely prefers situations where others are in charge and do the planning. Jackie needs help with the many important decisions in her life. This need is especially strong when she has any kind of problem at work or in her social life. At such times, she first calls her brother. If he is unavailable, she calls her mother to discuss the problem at length.

Jackie has a modest income as a junior-level attorney, but she is well on her way to a substantial estate on account of her brother's shrewd investments. When her father passed away, her brother moved into the slot of guardian and financial adviser to Jackie. Over the years, he has invested her savings, along with his own, in a variety of commercial real estate properties.

He handles all facets of the investments, including accounting and taxes. She usually takes a 5 or 10 percent position in buildings which he purchases with a few other friends. Her capital contributions to individual projects range from $5,000 to $15,000.

Jackie has been saving the positive cash flow from these investments and uses such funds and capital gains from closed-out partnerships for new projects. She justifiably has total confidence in her brother—his track record is excellent. He makes conservative investments which begin to generate income a year or two after their initiation. So far, several of their investments have been sold at handsome profits.

Jackie's dependent temperament combined with a fortunate set of circumstances explains her unusual investment success. She loves, trusts, and depends on, her brother. It so happens that he is a knowledgeable and savvy investor in real estate. So, Jackie has benefitted and will continue to benefit from this arrangement without quite realizing how fortunate she is.

Eric's situation provides a sharp contrast to that of Jackie's. He, too, has a dependent temperament and lives alone. His marginal income barely covers basic expenses which include a $1,050 monthly rental on a two-bedroom apartment.

Several years ago, Eric came across a three-bedroom house in a desirable location close to his office. He could have purchased it with $27,000 down and monthly mortgage payments of about $975 per month. It was obvious to him at the time that the property was selling at a discount to market value and that a minimal amount of restoration would increase its value considerably.

Eric, being dependent, needed to have someone with greater authority encourage him to make the purchase. He discussed the matter with his parents and they suggested his uncle who they felt was knowledgeable about construction. His uncle examined the house, discovered it needed a new roof, and advised Eric not to buy it.

Eric bypassed the opportunity and, within a year, escalating housing prices drove comparable homes beyond his financial reach. He now knows that he should have acted on his own judgment and purchased the particular house which currently is worth nearly three times as much. Had he done so, he now would have considerable financial security and a smaller after-tax housing expense.

The examples of Jackie and Eric might imply that a dependent person has equal chances of success and failure in turning to others for help with investments. Actually, Jackie provides a rare example of success. More often than not, arbitrarily selecting a financial adviser by turning to a person one likes and trusts results in a mediocre, or worse yet, disastrous investment performance. Most persons who happen to have provided good emotional support in the past are bound to be without any particular investment expertise and, therefore, to be ineffective as advisers on financial matters.

TYPICAL INVESTMENT STYLE OF THE DEPENDENT

What characteristics of dependent persons help explain their approaches to investments? Having a dependent temperament means being pleasant, arousable, and submissive. Dependent persons have positive social expectations and enjoy and value close relationships and social activities. Being submissive, they follow rather than lead, preferring to let others pave the way, give direction, or organize activities. They are suggestible and take on attitudes, opinions, and values of those they like, trust, and respect.

When they have problems, mishaps, failures, pains, illnesses, or anxieties, dependent persons are especially in need of help from others. They'll turn to the same familiar source for help repeatedly, but since usually this is not possible, they rely on any close friends, relatives, or even acquaintances, who happen to be accessible.

Dependent persons also lack the confidence or initiative to follow through on a suggested course of action independently and frequently need additional reassurance or ideas to proceed with a project they have initiated. This is how they give the impression of being demanding and clinging.

Being person-oriented, dependent individuals do not usually get their investment ideas from readings on the fundamentals of investing. Usually, there are limits to how much one can learn about investing from casual conversations and this lack of fundamental knowledge, since it further reduces confidence, aggravates dependent persons' problems in investing.

Those few dependent persons who invest in the stock or futures markets tend to rely on advice contained in various investment newsletters or the advice of their brokers. Indeed, they sometimes subscribe to several newsletters and hold accounts at a few brokerage houses so as to maximize the advice they get. To the dependent, such services seem sources of valuable "inside" tips.

Actually, the information contained in various publications or obtained from different brokers is likely to be contradictory and simply to generate additional uncertainty for the dependent. In this context, the investment actions of the dependent are determined by the most forceful and emotionally compelling suggestions. When their investments do badly, the dependent look outward rather than inward to diagnose the problem. Typically, they fail to examine their own investment methods and instead blame the advice they followed.

There are two important stages to investing. For the dependent, things can go wrong at either stage. First, is the period prior to commitment of funds to a particular property. This stage requires careful consideration of many available options, study of the relevant technical literature, and selection of an investment area and specific investment vehicle based on factors such as desired returns, risk, cash flow, and so forth.

Dependent persons usually bypass most of the necessary preparation at this stage by simply imitating a strong and persuasive other who seems to do well with investments or who gives the appearance of expertise. In this way, they do not usually get a chance to appraise the suitability of the particular investment to their own financial and emotional abilities.

The almost random way in which they select investments in the first stage creates an initial handicap which is accentuated during the second, post-commitment, stage. Having purchased a property (e.g., stock, bond, commodity, real estate, mutual fund), they must manage it and make additional purchase and sale decisions. The person who served as catalyst to initiate the investment may not be available regularly to provide advice or suggestions during this second stage. Alternatively, that source may himself encounter difficulties with his investments, express doubts about his earlier strategy, or move on to other unrelated investments. In any case, the dependent person is left stranded and his sense of security is shattered; he has no solid technical or emotional base to implement the investment strategy which was put into motion.

Lack of confidence may be tolerable as long as the investment does well. But, if it begins to do poorly, the emotional state associated with a dependent temperament (pleasant, arousable, submissive) together with stress generated by an investment that is doing poorly (strong displeasure and high arousal) results in feelings of displeasure, very high arousal, and submissiveness (i.e., discomfort, distress, anxiety, fear, or even terror or panic). We refer to this cluster of emotions as "anxiety" and recognize that it includes variations ranging from mild discomfort on to the extreme of panic, depending on the strength of emotions brought on by the investments themselves.

Persistent anxiety is psychologically devastating. Aside from the discomfort while one is awake, there is a good chance of insomnia. Frequent loss of sleep in turn results in additional tension and detracts from one's ability to think clearly. While feeling anxious, it is difficult to work effectively or to relate to others harmoniously and satisfactorily. Some physical outcomes of persistent anxiety are loss of appetite and sexual drive, perpetual exhaustion, and a variety of psychosomatic ailments. Someone suffering from anxiety is not a fun companion and instead can become a psychological burden to family and friends. All in all, anxiety brought on by investments can have overwhelming and negative psychological consequences in other areas of life.

Of all emotion states, anxiety is the most detrimental to one's ability to cope with difficult situations, such as, investments that are doing poorly. Normally, an investment strategy anticipates both positive and negative scenarios and is designed to yield a certain probable and positive end result averaged over the course of many ups and downs. Such a strategy helps one keep transitory problems in perspective and to weather difficult periods. When an investor is anxious, however, this perspective tends to be lost. Temporary difficulties assume exaggerated importance and emotions prevail over thought in determining decisions and actions. In this way, anxiety feeds on itself and drives the dependent person to extreme measures.

Investment plans are abandoned readily since there was no solid base for their selection in the first place. The investor haphazardly casts around for help, failing to consider and balance the many factors which go into obtaining useful advice from competent sources. Suggestions of a friend, relative, or casual acquaintance, or quotes from experts in financial magazines or newspapers can all trigger a change of plan.

The dangers (costs) of erratic changes are particularly great with highly "liquid" investments which are purchased and sold easily and quickly (e.g., stocks, bonds, commodities, options, financial futures). The dependent individual easily can sell such a disappointing holding, try out a different plan suggested by someone else, usually fail to benefit from the new plan, discard that, and so forth.

Progressive loss of capital and fear of additional losses usually deter the dependent from going too far in this way. Being submissive, they are more conservative and less risk-oriented than dominant persons. Unlike some dominant types who might go on and take additional risks, the dependent are likely to give up faster in defeat with smaller losses.

Even with small or moderate losses, though, the dependent learn to fear the class of investments which caused the losses. The trauma of losses plus associated feelings of anxiety and fear become deeply rooted and usually generalize to almost all investments involving risk. Such generalized fear leads the dependent to take shelter in the safest possible investment havens, such as savings accounts, and to blindly limit themselves to these for the rest of their lives.

THE PROCLIVITY OF THE DEPENDENT TO CONFORM

Dependent persons, insofar as they are submissive, tend to be timid and generally averse to risk taking. Unlike dominant persons, such as the exuberant, who are more adventuresome and risk-oriented in investing, submissive individuals, including the dependent, tend to be attracted to familiar and safe investments.

Considering this tendency of the dependent to be timid, how is it that they sometimes get involved with high-uncertainty investments? The answer requires an analysis of the phenomenon of conformity—the conditions under which we become susceptible to the influence of others.

All of us become more conforming, that is, more prone to follow someone else's suggestions or influence, to turn to others for guidance, to imitate others, or even to be manipulated when we feel highly aroused and submissive. This happens, for instance, when we try to

solve a difficult problem and cannot, must make a difficult purchase choice, or have to make any important
decision regarding two or more alternative actions where
the consequences of a wrong choice are costly.

Important choice points make us highly aroused because
we attempt a complex balancing of the pros and cons of
each avenue of action. There are many aspects of each
choice one must consider to make a decision. Thus, in
addition to complexity, there is considerable novelty,
and if the decision has to be made rapidly, then our
actions and thoughts involve fast changes.

*The more complicated a decision is and the faster it has
to be made, the more aroused one becomes.*

We feel submissive when we are in a situation we
cannot control. For instance, we feel submissive when
we must make a decision regarding something without
adequate knowledge, when we have a problem we cannot
master, or when we are in a setting where others dictate
what happens.

The third dimension of emotion, pleasure, also
comes into play during conformity. High arousal and
submissiveness increase our tendency to conform. But,
we are far more likely to conform to someone who is
pleasant rather than unpleasant. Also, of course, we conform more to individuals who are dominant, such as
authority figures, high status persons, or experts.

*In sum, emotional conditions of high arousal, submis-
siveness, and pleasure, generated by situations and others,
increase the likelihood of conformity or susceptibility to influence.*

This background is essential for understanding
which temperament types are the most conforming. In
analogy to individuals who are temporarily made to feel
aroused and submissive by circumstances, *persons who are
temperamentally arousable and submissive show a greater
across-the-board inclination to conform. Thus, two of our
temperament types, the dependent and the anxious, are expected to be highly susceptible to the influence of others—par-*

ticularly the influence of those whom they like (pleasant source) and respect (pleasant plus dominant source). Conversely, unarousable and dominant (relaxed or disdainful) individuals are least likely, in general, to be influenced, guided, or manipulated by others.

Our discussion of conformity in general, and emotional elements of decisions in particular, has important bearing for understanding a person's vulnerability to random external influences in investing. We now know the emotional circumstances under which people relinquish their internal standards and self direction.

While feeling aroused and submissive, investment decisions tend to be influenced unduly and in helter-skelter fashion by persons or sources that happen to be present and are authoritative or compelling. Analogously, arousable, and submissive (dependent, anxious) temperament types are more likely to have their investment pathways changed almost randomly depending on the compelling figures or sources which happen to be present at different times. In contrast, unarousable and dominant (relaxed, disdainful) temperament types have greater immunity to external influence and are better able to adhere to their own plans of action.

CONFORMING TO THE CROWD

A major compelling source of influence for everyone, particularly the dependent or anxious, is the crowd. Investments, like clothing styles, automobile brands, and diets, come into, and fall out of, fashion. Mob psychology is a potent influence in accentuating (price) swings of the pendulum in every investment area.

The real estate craze of the late 1980s began slowly and gradually in that decade, with only a small segment of the investment public participating in the mid 1980s. As prices rose and success stories were told and retold in personal contacts and through every conceivable news medium, real estate investing picked up an increasingly larger following.

Once the momentum (the pendulum swing) was underway, it became easier to make money investing in real estate because demand increased at an accelerating pace. Near the end of the swing, the investment medium was infused with mob psychology. Very large numbers of investors, including novice speculators, were convinced this was the sure way to make plenty of money rapidly and competed indiscriminately with one another to purchase real estate, thereby driving up prices.

Massive psychological forces come into play in speculative markets and near market tops. When prices increase rapidly near the top of frenzied markets, it is difficult not to be aware of what is happening and not to be tempted to take advantage of a seemingly easy money-making scheme. One reads about success stories, hears friends talk about their particular investment coups, and discovers how easy it is to participate.

The attraction is greatest for temperamentally dependent and conformist persons—those who derive gratification from being with others, belonging to groups, being accepted, and having attitudes, interests, hobbies, or avocations similar to those of their peers.

The mob scene and the uniform strong conviction of the mob entice the typically timid dependent or anxious to plunge into speculative (high-uncertainty) investments. The larger the mob or crowd and the stronger its collective voice, the greater is the temptation.

Unfortunately, a very strong crowd conviction is required to tempt dependent and anxious persons to abandon caution and to enter the fray. They thus enter highly speculative and dangerous markets at or near price peaks, since that is where the crowd is most persuasive.

However, prices peak when the conviction of the crowd is the strongest. At the peak, most potential speculators have used up the bulk of their financial resources to make purchases and significant additional funds are no longer available to help raise prices.

Highly popular and speculative investment markets should therefore ring loud warning bells for the dependent (and the anxious). Dependent persons need to be attuned to, and vigilant about, their heightened vulnerability to investment fashions. Indeed, more generally, they should recognize that they are prone to find high-uncertainty investments tempting only when the latter seem safe—and this is a contradiction and a dangerous trap.

INVESTMENT GUIDELINES FOR THE DEPENDENT

Awareness of the "pull" of the crowd in speculative markets, together with knowledge of one's own tendency to be dependent and conforming, is useful to safeguard against the massive psychological forces at work in popular markets. Dependent persons, then, can try to check temptations to conform by learning about the key indicators of frenzied, speculative markets and by making determined efforts to shun such markets.

Aside from avoiding popular, speculative markets, dependent persons can be watchful of markets in which they hold investments and which turn popular. In such instances, a useful guideline is to refrain strictly from increasing the dollar amounts invested. In this way, the percent of capital and disposable income invested in a specific market remains at a reasonable level—one that is determined under normal conditions prior to popularity and, therefore, one which is dictated by more detached and less emotional considerations.

Investment strategies recommended for the arousable (Chapter 5) and the submissive (Chapter 6) are especially suited to the dependent and are worth reviewing at this point. For instance, one idea is to rely on professionally managed investments instead of trying to invest for oneself. A large variety of such investment options are available and cover a broad spectrum from low to high uncertainty.

Once dependent individuals accept the premise that they are better off having their funds professionally handled, much of the complexity, bewilderment, "noise," and traps associated with investing is avoided. Only two basic decisions are required—selecting the level of investment uncertainty and picking a management team.

If dependent individuals invest for themselves, they should select low-uncertainty investments. Examples of low-uncertainty investments are bank deposits paying fixed interest, U.S. Treasury bills and notes, money market funds, or U.S. Treasury bonds that can be held to maturity, thereby guaranteeing recovery of capital plus steady interest income.

When, on the other hand, dependent persons use the services of professionals to invest their funds, they can withstand higher levels of uncertainty because they would not be coping directly and actively with the investments. They, for instance, may select closed-end corporate bond funds, municipal bond funds of high safety ratings, or mutual funds which emphasize preservation of capital with some potential for capital gains, such as, funds invested in high quality convertible bonds. In all these instances, selection of the appropriate fund can be made by researching the records of various funds in each class.

Fund statistics are available through financial publications and expertise is not required to select funds with the desired characteristics and proven records of excellence. Much of the selection work can be done by calling securities brokers and requesting information on the records of various funds. A few hours spent in reading and a few more phone calls to brokers for additional clarification should help narrow down the selection. During this search, investors would do well to solicit factual information, such as fund performance statistics, and to clearly state, and adhere to, their investment goals.

THE CONTRARIAN APPROACH

In closing, it is useful to note the "contrarian approach," a school of investment philosophy that is diametrically opposite to the natural and intuitive investment choices of the dependent. In the contrarian approach, highly popular investments in the portfolio are sold to the crowd which surges to buy them at unreasonably high prices and highly unpopular investments are purchased when they are ignored or shunned by the crowd.

Indeed, some shrewd investment professionals who regularly come into contact with a wide range of investors have learned to use a limited variant of the contrarian approach. Their intimate knowledge of the performance records of many investors helps them identify certain investors as "negative indicators." These are investors who typically misjudge short-term market turns or who seem to invariably make the wrong choice from among highly touted investment issues. Investors who serve as negative indicators have highly sensitive antennae and rush to those segments of the market where the baits are most tempting. They thus purchase when the knowledgeable sell or sell when the experts buy. Professionals who can identify such flesh-and-blood negative indicators benefit from their trading patterns by simply doing exactly the opposite.

A few prominent advocates of the contrarian approach in the stock market take the idea to its logical extreme. In making selections for their portfolios, they seek stocks that not only are ignored, but rather actively hated, by the crowd. The underlying assumption is that when the broad mass of investment public, including professionals, actively dislikes stocks in a particular industry group, the prices of those stocks are bound to have been pounded down beyond reason under the pressure of excessive negative emotionality. Thus, unemotional purchase of those highly unpopular stocks at bargain-basement prices, together with the patience and monetary resources to wait out the period of unpopularity, results in investment gains that are significantly higher than those achieved by most.

Chapter 10

The Relaxed

Jasen is in his sixties and has spent most of his working life in the securities business. During his early days as a stockbroker, and at almost the very end of a prolonged stock market decline that had lasted several years, he was witness to a most dramatic event.

The extended bear market had been extremely demoralizing for stockbrokers. They first had witnessed their active customers suffer substantial losses and stop trading. Even their more steadfast customers sold their stocks and stopped trading once the decline persisted for a year or two. By this time, the brokerage business began to suffer, commission income was reduced drastically, and stockbrokers were laid off. As the decline persisted, matters became increasingly bleak—more customers sold, taking huge losses, more friends were laid off, and work days were generally slow and uninteresting.

Jasen recalls these endless slow and painful days and the seemingly interminable decline. He remembers the feeling of despair which pervaded during the final two weeks of the bear market.

It was during those final days of the decline when Jasen saw a shabbily dressed man walk into the office carrying a suitcase. The visitor's interaction with one of the senior partners of the firm made it clear he was well known and respected. The suitcase bulged with cash and the client was there to use all the money to buy stocks.

He had brought along a long shopping list and spent the day at the office filling orders.

Jasen remembers that day very well, not only because of the general inactivity at the office, but because of the poor state of the economy and the shortage of cash accompanying it. The sight of a man with a suitcase full of money was most unusual. But, this was hardly as dramatic as the apparent coincidence of that event with a very sharp turnaround in stock prices a few days later.

There are two impressive qualities to note here. First, is the patience to wait out a decline of several years while having a tremendous hoard of cash and despite the constant temptation to buy brought on by progressive price drops. Second, is the resolve and confidence to commit all this cash at a juncture when the economy and the market look their very dismal worst and when feelings of doom and gloom prevail.

Aside from obvious technical expertise, a person who is capable psychologically of such a feat is most probably unarousable and dominant. It takes low arousability to devise a long-term investment plan and adhere to it without wavering despite innumerable temptations and then to act when most are paralyzed with despair or fear. It also takes dominance to act independently and with confidence, moving against massive social forces which discourage almost every investor.

A relaxed temperament constellation includes these two qualities along with pleasantness. It not only is the healthiest temperament, but is the most conducive to investment success as well.

Stress generated by problems of everyday living brings on psychological and physical ailments. As we have seen, the uncertainty of investing also generates stress. Since the relaxed are pleasant, unarousable, and dominant, they have a natural immunity to the displeasure, arousal, and submissiveness generated by stress. Thus, although the relaxed are also affected by stress, they, compared with other temperament types, feel its effect to a lesser degree. *By virtue of their high tolerance for pain, discomfort, and anxiety, and greater stamina and resistance to fatigue, the relaxed are ideal candidates for high-stress jobs and activities, including high-uncertainty investing.*

THE CASES OF TOM AND PETER

A couple of personality sketches are needed to illustrate the relaxed temperament. Tom is a soldier in a field of combat. He can nap when a lull in the fighting permits him to take a rest. He wakes up from such naps feeling refreshed and calm, while his companions stay awake performing a variety of mindless chores. Sleep is beyond question for them as they are too wound up. Tom also sleeps well at nights while several others suffer from insomnia, sleep poorly or restlessly, or have frequent nightmares.

After several weeks of combat duty, Tom has a definite psychological edge over his companions. His ability to sleep well at nights and to take occasional naps during the day help his body unwind and regenerate. He wakes up calm, alert, and full of energy while his mates are beginning to show the cumulative effects of sleeplessness and inadequate rest. They suffer from chronic fatigue, tension, edginess, or the jitters, and are unable to concentrate for prolonged periods. They also have physical symptoms such as headaches, digestive difficulties, colds, flues, and even more serious physical ailments which make them unfit for combat.

It is evident that when his company actively engages the enemy, Tom's chances of survival are greater than that of his mates. He has psychological reserves which enable him to generate and sustain the very high levels of arousal required by combat. He can be active physically, move fast and nimbly, be alert and watchful, act to safeguard himself and his companions, and he can maintain this high-arousal state for long periods of time.

In contrast, his mates who have depleted their physical and psychological resources have difficulty generating the high levels of physical and mental arousal that are necessary for combat and their own security. They are tired, tense, less alert to changing conditions, and more inclined to make mistakes or to have accidents and injuries.

High-uncertainty investments often require many of the psychological resources and skills demanded in combat situations. In comparison with other temperament types, relaxed persons like Tom respond to the stress of high-uncertainty investments with the least anxiety.

Peter trades in commodities. He began his career as an exchange clerk in his twenties. Now, at the age of 34, he makes as much as $50 million a year by trading commodities for his own account. He uses several television monitors to track ever-changing commodity prices. He trades daily in transactions worth tens of millions.

He makes split-second decisions to purchase or sell gold, for instance, that could lose him millions and yet is able to do so with as much ease as it would take you and I to order a meal. Unlike other high-powered traders who often rely on drugs to keep up the required inordinately high pace, Peter only uses vitamins to supplement his diet.

Peter's manner conveys calm confidence. He is not a slave to his work and takes off a week or two periodically to get away from the turmoil. A good part of his success hinges on his ability to rest instead of staying wound up at all times. This ability to be somewhat detached while in the midst of turmoil is a characteristic of relaxed persons.

A related characteristic is the ability to physically and psychologically break away from the fray and give oneself a chance to recuperate and regenerate much-needed resources. Other traders cannot seem to get away from the hectic trading atmosphere even during meals or while socializing in the evenings. Not so with Peter;

at the end of the workday, he leaves work, leaving behind most work-related thoughts and concerns.

GENERAL CHARACTERISTICS OF THE RELAXED

One's approach to investments, like one's approach to work, play, and socializing is a reflection of one's temperament. It, therefore, helps to understand a person's investment style when we have a broader idea of their life style.

The most important aspect of our lives is the way we relate to others. Relaxed persons have positive social expectations: they expect interactions with others to be fun and rewarding and value close relationships and friendships. Their manner in social situations is calm and comfortable, instead of high-paced or highly active. Unlike exuberant and dependent persons, they are less involved with others; they do not need social contacts as much and are more detached and appraising in their relationships.

Their dominance is manifested in the control they exert over their personal affairs, surroundings, plans, and work. Their influence in social situations is subtle and less apparent in comparison with that of exuberant persons.

Also, relaxed persons control social or work relationships that are significant to themselves instead of being indiscriminately controlling in most relationships. Thus, control is focused upon their own affairs, their careers, and strivings for high achievement in social activities, sports and hobbies, and investments.

Our discussion of conformity in the preceding chapter showed that relaxed (and disdainful) individuals are the least conforming or susceptible to others' influence. They plan important social, work-related, or recreational activities independently. When long-range plans require persistence and psychological stamina in the face of frequent adversity or failure, they retain their internal bearings and do not helplessly and indiscriminately turn to others for guidance.

PHOBIA AND COUNTER-PHOBIA

The notion of "counter-phobia" has been used in the clinical literature to describe those who seek situations or activities that scare or threaten most. Two of our temperament types, the exuberant and the relaxed, help characterize this interesting concept.

Exuberant persons, as we have seen, are risk oriented and engage in activities in ways as to increase excitement and thrill. If they ski, they are likely to ski advanced slopes. In any sport, they are likely to take more chances and to strive for pizazz instead of taking a cautious and calculating route. In anything they do, the exuberant would almost seem to prefer spectacular failure to mediocre success achieved through plodding and monotony.

The exuberant, insofar as they take on dangerous situations or prefer extreme and risky activities, represent one variant of counter-phobic. However, the relaxed possess all essential qualities of the true counter-phobic.

Phobia, after all, refers to irrational fear. And, a relaxed temperament involves emotional characteristics that are the exact opposites of fear. The true counter-phobic has a better chance than most to deal successfully with a dangerous or highly stressful situation. Such a person does not approach demanding situations with spectacular flourish, but rather calmly, with deliberation, great tolerance of pain and discomfort, ability to delay gratification, and persistence in the face of repeated failures. Thus, unlike the exuberant who "goes down in flames," the relaxed emerges as victor.

INVESTING BY THE RELAXED

In line with the broad characteristics of their temperament, relaxed persons approach investments planfully and systematically, instead of impulsively. Being dominant, they develop their own investment plans after reading the pertinent literature and discussing their ideas with knowledgeable persons.

Once they select a particular investment strategy, they initiate the plan on a small scale to test it, instead of plunging ahead at the start with large or burdensome financial commitments. Following a period of testing and adjustments of strategy, as they become more confident about the soundness of their approach, they gradually commit larger sums to the investments.

Careful planning, caution, testing, readjustment of strategies, and gradually increasing financial commitment all help to instill confidence in a long-term investment plan. Thus, when they experience temporary setbacks in their investments, relaxed persons are able to retain their confidence and longer-term perspective. In this way, they do not react with extreme anxiety or fear to temporary reversals and do not "crack" and bail out of investments at inopportune times. Instead, they ride out difficult periods while maintaining a balanced focus on the entire sequence of ups and downs that was anticipated.

The relaxed are not infallible and, like others, can get into poor investment situations. In such instances, they do not have much difficulty in closing out loss-prone positions and moving on to other, more profitable trades. Unlike the hostile, anxious, or dependent, relaxed individuals more easily overcome negative feelings generated by investment losses. They do not brood about losses or carry the negative emotions to their work or home.

Another important characteristic of the relaxed is their ability to maintain an emotional distance from investment markets. When they are involved in the faster-paced stock or futures markets, they generally avoid making trading decisions on the spur of the moment while prices are fluctuating. Instead, they probably adhere to a regular schedule of study and preparation when markets are closed. During these periods, they catch up on background reading, update information they need for their current investments, explore new investment opportunities, and make trading decisions.

Exploring investment options and making investment decisions when markets are closed and during periods when one can relax and take a more detached attitude are important ingredients of success. This ability to distance comes naturally to the relaxed as well as to the disdainful described in a subsequent chapter.

Douglas, the sociology professor, in "Cases" provides a good example of the methodical, patient, confident, and independent investment style of relaxed individuals. Douglas began with minimal capital and invested it only after several months of concentrated study of a particular stock that had been brought to his attention. He committed money to the stock when he had determined a safe purchase price and after he had verified that moves of the stock confirmed his expectations based on its long-term historical price-volume charts. He purchased and sold the same issue over a period of several years, always waiting patiently for correct conditions to prevail so he could act on a predetermined decision. His patient, systematic approach to investing in the stock market made it possible for Douglas to accumulate capital at an incredibly fast pace.

Douglas intuitively selected the stock market, a high-uncertainty investment area. Being relaxed in temperament, he was ambitious and selected risky investments that have the potential to provide greater returns.

There is not much advice to be given relaxed individuals about how they might overcome temperament-related handicaps in investing. Nevertheless, sometimes due to family history, upbringing and values, or educational limitations, relaxed individuals confine themselves to low-uncertainty, low-return investments such as savings accounts. In such cases, awareness of the advantageous qualities of their temperament can encourage them to experiment with somewhat higher-level uncertainty investments. They may, thus, discover a facility with investments which they did not know they possessed.

Lest the reader is left with the mistaken impression that relaxed persons are bound invariably to be successful as investors, it is important to note that all investments, particularly high-uncertainty ones, carry risks of failure. Our discussion of the beneficial temperament characteristics of relaxed persons implies these *risks of losses are lower for relaxed, in comparison with other, temperament types.*

Also, as we shall see (Chapter 16), investment success is affected in important ways by one's life circumstances. A relaxed person may have a highly stressful job or family life. Stress generated by these situational and incidental sources can be a detriment to investment success, despite advantages of a relaxed temperament.

Generally, in investing, we must consider the advantages and handicaps due to temperament in addition to those generated by life circumstances. Analysis of these combined forces provides a complete view of the psychological factors which influence one's particular manner of investing and one's chances of success. We have so far focused on the influences of temperament, while incidentally providing the foundation for understanding the emotional effects of life circumstances. Once all temperament types have been examined, it will be an easy matter to show parallel influences of life circumstances on likelihood of investment success.

Chapter 11
The Docile

Jane has been working as an attorney for the last twenty years. Whenever senior partners at her firm have a particularly sticky legal problem, they turn to Jane for help. The more complex and messier a legal situation is, the more she excels in formulating a straightforward solution. Even though she earns far less than she is worth, Jane is happy with her job and gets along well with her coworkers.

At home, as at work, Jane defers major decisions to others; usually, her husband. In social situations, she is pleasant, friendly but not talkative, and calm and comfortable. She is content to let her friends schedule their social activities together. She participates easily in different situations and enjoys herself and her companions.

Jane has been inattentive to investments. Over the years, her savings consistently have gone into a variety of time deposits. Considering taxes and inflation, she probably has lost purchasing power, despite the accumulated and considerably larger dollar value of her deposits.

GENERAL CHARACTERISTICS OF THE DOCILE

Jane has a "docile" temperament. Her quiet and likeable qualities are characteristic of this temperament. Since the docile are pleasant, unarousable, and submissive, they resemble the relaxed, differing insofar as they are submissive instead of dominant. As with relaxed persons, they value friendships but are not excessively needy of social contacts. Also, when socializing, they are not highly active but can stay in the background and enjoy the company of others in a detached way.

The docile resemble the dependent (who are pleasant, arousable, and submissive), but differ from the latter in important ways because they are less arousable. Generally, a person's susceptibility to influence increases with greater arousal and submissiveness. Lower arousability of the docile, compared with the dependent, makes the docile less conformist or suggestible — less prone to be influenced by actions, opinions, and values of others.

The docile, being less emotional and more placid than the dependent, are less desperate or frantic and more sensible and objective in seeking assistance when they are confronted with interpersonal problems, job-related difficulties, mishaps, accidents, setbacks, or illnesses. As a consequence, they have more success in obtaining competent information, advice, or help and in coping with daily difficulties.

Compared with the dependent, the docile are more tolerant of discomfort, pain, or difficulties encountered at work or at home, because they do not feel as anxious. Docile persons, thus, manifest many strengths of the relaxed. Like relaxed persons, they are calm and level-headed in difficult or stressful situations. But compared with relaxed persons, they are less determined or stubborn, less ambitious, less confident, and more likely to seek guidance from others to initiate and carry through their plans.

INVESTING BY THE DOCILE

A docile temperament is clearly advantageous in investing, even though it is handicapped by submissiveness.

Typically, submissive persons lack confidence in their own judgments and decisions and rely on others for guidance, even when these others lack expertise to give useful help. However, of the four submissive temperament types (dependent, docile, anxious, bored), the docile, since they are pleasant and unarousable, have the fewest investment problems because of how they use outside help.

Although, like other submissive persons, they rely on outside advice and direction, they are more discriminating and thorough in searching for competent and balanced guidance. Since they are better prepared and begin with carefully formulated and advantageous strategies, they are more likely to adhere to their investment programs despite temporary market reversals and adversities. They are less fickle or capricious in changing investment strategies mid-course.

Investment success involves a proper meshing of the emotional impact of investments and emotional characteristics (strengths and weaknesses) of investors. Some investors take on investments they are unable to handle because of their characteristic inability to cope with difficult or stressful situations—they take on too much uncertainty. Others do not do as well as they might because they take on too little investment uncertainty, even though their temperaments would allow them to handle more.

The docile, with their characteristic pleasant and unarousable dispositions, are capable of coping with significant levels of stress and uncertainty. Nevertheless, being submissive, they lack confidence and ambition and sometimes are drawn to mundane, low-uncertainty investments which only produce meager results.

There are occasions during our lifetimes when we have the necessary financial resources and are presented with unusual investment opportunities. These rare lifetime opportunities can produce excellent results with only small increases in risk and discomfort. Absence of confidence or adventuresome spirit leads the docile to make only half-hearted stabs at such investments. They participate, however, if they get the right kind of timely encouragement.

Generally, the docile do not do as well in investing as the relaxed or disdainful because, unlike the latter two, they lack confidence. The docile, then, can be said to be underachievers in investing—they settle for goals lower than ones they can achieve.

It is important for docile persons to become aware of their characteristic emotional strengths and to examine their investment histories. They might recall opportunities which they rejected and how they would have fared had they taken advantage of those opportunities. Specifically, they should write out a list of such opportunities, reasons for rejecting each, and the approximate appreciation (or returns) of those investments.

Such a list will reveal a tendency to stay with less challenging and comfortable investments. They will note a tendency to follow family traditions and to hang on to trust-fund managers, stocks, or bonds which have been passed down. The list also will reveal a proclivity to rely on guidance from relatives or long-time counselors who consistently discourage selection of moderate- or high-uncertainty investments. Examining the list of bypassed investment opportunities will help develop greater self-awareness and should encourage closer and more careful study of upcoming investments. Nevertheless, the docile, like other submissive persons, must be attuned to the dangers of highly popular, speculative markets and refrain from participation in these.

Jane, for instance, because of her substantial financial resources, is bound to have future chances to make highly beneficial investments, without getting involved in frantic mob-dominated markets. Once she becomes aware of her temperament and discovers the reasons for her uncalled-for conservatism, she is likely to examine upcoming investment opportunities with more care and to pursue them with greater vigor. When she finds herself acting doubtfully or half-heartedly, she will recognize this as a byproduct of her temperament rather than attribute it to low merits of an investment. She will then have a better chance to overcome her emotional barriers and commit to an investment that makes good financial and economic sense.

Chapter 12

Investments for the Hostile

Lorna is a 36-year-old divorcee. She lives in an expensive home which she owns outright and is supported mainly by alimony and child-support payments.

With casual acquaintances, Lorna appears very intelligent and socially skillful, but somewhat reserved. Those who get to know her better discover that she spends most of her time alone and only has one or two close friends. They also find her to be very rigid. She has most definite likes and dislikes, actually many more dislikes than likes, and takes offense quickly when her friends or companions fail to consider these.

One can offend Lorna readily without knowing. It is not unusual for a companion to find her in a negative, highly reserved, incommunicative, and generally defensive mood. After an hour or two, the companion may discover she was upset because she thought he did not approve of her dress, her hairdo, or that he was not friendly enough when he greeted her.

Lorna does not tolerate any kind of criticism from friends or relatives. When she senses any hint of disapproval, she initially reacts with moodiness while she ruminates about what the criticism means and how she should get back at the offender. In the absence of communication, her imagination gets carried away. When eventually she explodes with anger and accusations, she is extremely persistent and devastating in her attack, demanding total subjugation.

Lorna demands absolute, unqualified approval from others; otherwise they do not qualify as true friends. And, she often is suspicious of others' motives and is prepared for the worst. On the rare occasions when she works, she becomes obsessed with some of her coworkers who she thinks are trying to take credit for the work she does.

Lorna also has frequent aggressive and violent fantasies. In congested traffic, she likes to imagine having a tractor-like vehicle to drive over automobiles which block her way. She keeps a pistol close at hand near her bed and has a plan on how to use it if a burglar were to break in at night.

A few years ago, Lorna came into a sizeable inheritance. She decided she would invest the money in the stock market and began to study the subject. She was very thorough in her studies and must have perused as many as 75 volumes in the course of a year. Among various schools of thought she read about, she liked the idea of buying stocks that were undervalued relative to basic assets and long-term earning potential.

According to this approach, aberrations in various segments of the economy or the stock market create conditions whereby stocks of some sound and asset-rich companies temporarily fall out of favor. One can purchase these when they are out of favor and, therefore, undervalued and hold them for a few years until economic conditions change and their earning potential becomes apparent. At that time, demand for the stocks increases and prices rise.

The investment strategy is sound and works well for those who correctly can select undervalued situations, hold on to these patiently and through periods when they might become even more undervalued, and sell when the stocks are in vogue and overpriced. Several publications research undervalued stocks and Lorna uses these to select a handful to purchase and hold at any given time. Her selections have been fine, but she has failed to benefit from her work and her investments. In fact, she shows a small percentage loss of her capital over the past few years.

Lorna's choice of investment strategy is incompatible with her hostile temperament. Stocks that are cheap and undervalued can stay that way for years and even get cheaper. The necessary psychological ingredients of success, therefore, are great confidence in one's choices and even greater patience, tolerance for frustration and discomfort, and ability to delay gratification.

Lorna has the confidence but lacks the remaining essentials. Typically, she makes a purchase and holds on through a few months while the stock has insignificant fluctuations in value. During this period, she initially loses interest in the issue. But as time goes on, she loses patience and tolerance. She becomes exasperated, angered, and even enraged by the failure of the stock to please and reward her for her effort and sacrifice.

Finally, during a particularly frustrating period when other pressures lower Lorna's threshold to pain and irritation, she impulsively sells the stock in disgust. Sometimes this happens while she watches the ticker tape and observes other issues moving up rapidly while her stocks remain inactive. Later, while in a calmer mood, she regrets those moments of passion and irrationality.

At times, Lorna manages to hold on to a stock through thick and thin and it finally begins to show a profit. Even with a small profit, Lorna becomes obsessed with the idea of selling. It is almost as if she has learned to dislike the stock for disappointing her in the past and cannot wait to be rid of it.

On occasion, a year or two after selling a stock, Lorna finds it appreciating significantly. This reassures her that she can pick undervalued situations. So, she continues to employ the strategy despite her inability to make it pay.

GENERAL CHARACTERISTICS OF THE HOSTILE

Lorna has a somewhat extreme form of the "hostile" (unpleasant, arousable, dominant) temperament. Hostile temperament is at the core of a variety of seemingly different personality types. In the psychological literature, some of these are described as rigid, inflexible, closed rather than open, defensive, aggressive, authoritarian, or narcissistic. Some neurotic cases are referred to as "obsessive-compulsive" where the expression of aggression is indirect and subtle. More extreme, psychotic, forms are labeled "paranoid schizophrenia." Another highly disturbed variety of hostile temperament is found among habitual and impulsively violent criminals.

We all encounter minor mishaps, delays and obstructions, and exasperating encounters or failures in our daily lives. What differentiates the hostile is their extreme emotional response to such situations—*the more hostile the individual, the more extreme, overt, and inappropriate the negative emotional reaction.* Situations which elicit mild irritation and silence from others, evoke open criticism, sarcasm, derogation, disgust, seething anger, tirades, threats, or physical violence from the hostile. The latter usually lack control over expression of their anger and are likely to blurt out their disenchantment or complaints or to lash out impulsively and violently.

Several common themes run through the lives of hostile persons. Negative social expectations associated with an unpleasant temperament take on a special slant in such individuals. They generally are mistrustful and suspicious of others and expect other persons, organizations, or social institutions to be malicious and to harm them. As a defense against these expectations, the hostile tend to be guarded and secretive. They also readily strike out in retaliation to negative insinuations, insults, derogatory statements, rejection, or malice, often imagined or exaggerated out of proportion.

When the hostile feel discomfort, failure, or pain, they hold others', rather than their own, actions responsible for these feelings. Given this perception, they retaliate with aggression designed to hurt, damage, or destroy the sources of their misery.

More subtly, the hostile often try to impose their attitudes and values on others. Having others conform and submit to their ways reduces chances of disagreements and irritation and is soothing to the hostile.

The tendency of the hostile to want to subjugate others mentally and/or physically is epitomized in the megalomaniac conquerors of the past and rabid political extremists of today. It is highlighted also in the religious fanatic and the proselytizer bent on changing society's ways through inculcation of "correct" beliefs and behaviors, elimination of "undesirable" ones, and imposition of stricter laws for all.

The hostile have difficulty forming warm or loving relationships. The close relationships they have tend to involve secretiveness, suspicion, mistrust, disagreements, altercations, rejections, threats, violent conflicts, separations, and periods of quiet rage or hatred.

INVESTING BY THE HOSTILE

Hostile persons do very poorly at investing. The only temperament type to do worse is the anxious. Investment is a two-step process: preparation and research before making a commitment and consistent adherence to a plan of action once money is invested. The hostile err at both stages, with their worst errors occurring at the second stage. Lorna is somewhat an exception in that she prepares adequately in the first stage with her reading and research. Unlike Lorna, the majority of hostile persons are less careful in making an initial commitment—they tend to be impulsive and emotional in choosing their investments. Their poor planning reduces their chances of success and increases probabilities of failure later on.

Investment pitfalls of the hostile are analyzed as follows. Before an investment is made and in the absence of pressure, the prospects seem exciting, invigorating, and a source of hope. Planning to invest, then, is pleasant and arousing. Combine this with the temperament of hostile individuals (unpleasant, arousable, dominant), and the result is moderate pleasure, very high arousal, and dominance. (Note that the externally induced pleasure outweighs the temperament-related displeasure.) The resulting emotional configuration is reminiscent of the exuberant and, indeed, at the planning stage, the hostile behave very much like the exuberant. They usually act impulsively and make commitments only after superficial study.

When things go wrong with an investment, feelings of displeasure, high arousal, and submissiveness result. This effect, combined with the emotional components of a hostile temperament, results in extreme displeasure, very high arousal, and moderate submissiveness, that is, anxiety. (Note that the externally induced submissiveness outweighs the temperament-related dominance.)

The hostile, however, being characteristically dominant, will often transform this anxiety to anger by asserting control (i.e., dominance) over such investments. This control is illusory, however, and is achieved usually in liquid markets with unthinking sales of the troublesome investments. Thus, insistence on control over an investment through its sale results in, possibly unnecessary, losses.

If, on the other hand, the hostile manage to avoid irrational actions designed to achieve control, they then must suffer high levels of anxiety induced by high-uncertainty investments. This anxiety narrows their perspectives, making it difficult for them to judge complex situations in a balanced way and to arrive at profitable investment decisions.

In more extreme cases, hostile temperament takes on the colorings of paranoia. Those in this category who are involved with stocks or futures typically are drawn to ideas that markets are controlled and manipulated by powerful, sinister forces. Investors who espouse such beliefs spend most of their efforts trying to detect what the "evil doers" are up to. Extensive preoccupations along these lines typically are accompanied by highly charged emotionality and do not include constructive investment plans. Instead, they are wasteful, continually ignite anger, and serve to assign blame for failure to external, unknown forces.

Sometimes, the hostile, as in Lorna's case, hold on to an investment through a period of mediocre performance and then become impatient with it as it recovers and shows a small gain. They then sell to give vent to accumulated resentment—almost as if to get even. Walter, a retired contractor, provides an example of this phenomenon. In the mid sixties, he joined forces with two close friends and purchased two apartment buildings. Walter was the general manager of the partnership, had been the decisive factor in the purchase, and oversaw the daily management and accounting. He received a small management fee.

The partnership held the properties through seven years of mediocre real estate markets. The investment was a continuing irritant to Walter since it tied up most of his capital and only produced a meager income.

In the early seventies, real estate prices firmed and then began to show signs of an extended recovery. As soon as Walter detected a chance to sell the properties and regain his invested capital with a small gain, he convinced his partners to sell. They sold both buildings in 1973. Had they held on for an additional six or seven years, they could have obtained at least three times as much for the properties, with each partner netting close to one million dollars. Instead, Walter, totally disenchanted with real estate, placed his part of the proceeds from the sale in a savings account. By then, he had no tolerance for high-risk investments and wanted something secure and trouble-free. Unfortunately for him, inflation accelerated in the latter part of the seventies and his interest income was more than offset by losses in purchasing power of his capital.

OBSESSIVE-COMPULSIVES

As already noted, the obsessive-compulsive personality identified by Freud is a variant of the hostile temperament. One source of failure for obsessive-compulsives in investing is their rigid and inflexible attitudes toward various investment areas. Some examples are firmly entrenched beliefs about real estate as the all-time investment of choice, a life-long love of gold, holding cash at all times and failing to take advantage of bargain prices during severe recessionary periods, or the belief that there will be endless inflation without any possibility of deflation.

Of the various temperament types, the hostile are most likely to become enamored in this way with a particular investment or with an investment philosophy that dictates all investment tactics. Such inflexibility precludes consideration of more promising alternatives under differing economic conditions.

Another reason obsessive-compulsives lose in investing is because they tend to be stingy and frequently are attracted to investments that seem cheap; for instance, low-priced stocks or residential properties in undesirable locations. But, unless they are fortunate and purchase stocks, commodities, or real estate that are truly undervalued, their inexpensive purchases get even cheaper. Obsessive-compulsives fail to learn from past experiences and repeat old mistakes. They, thus, continually gravitate to investments which seem cheap and yet generate losses.

Buying cheaply does not always lead to losses. Indeed, savvy professionals such as Warren Buffet, a disciple of Benjamin Graham, have shown it is extremely worthwhile to invest in undervalued situations. Such professionals, however, have extensive resources which permit them to scrutinize fundamentals of companies, verify reported statements of assets and liabilities, and estimate future earnings prospects. Few individual investors have the resources or specialized knowledge to apply these techniques in search of companies or investments with undervalued assets. Instead, when individuals, due to their emotional characteristics, are drawn to investments that seem cheap (but are justifiably so), they lose.

A second, though less common, variant of the compulsive investor almost seems determined to lose the money he invests. Such a person usually is caught up in a dominance conflict with his mate or another family member and, generally, is forced into a subordinate role relative to the stronger relative. He compensates for this by using his income passive-aggressively and as a last resort to assert some measure of control and independence.

The compulsive knows the money he earns and brings home will be spent according to the needs and wishes of the other, more dominant, person in the family. He, thus, frequently and hastily commits his wages to investments of his choice before the other has a chance to dictate how the money is spent.

Hasty and careless investments of this kind usually lead to losses, but nevertheless provide the compulsive investor with some psychological benefits. He gets his way. He also gets some satisfaction and excitement fantasizing about positive outcomes of his investments. Finally, he derives gratification from the way his losses cause frustration and aggravation to the more dominant family member. Incidentally, this pattern is also found among some compulsive gamblers.

IDENTIFYING ONE'S INVESTMENT PATTERNS

Because of their capacity to generate large investment losses, it is important for hostile persons to become aware of their investment patterns and pitfalls. If such individuals are determined to choose high-uncertainty investments (involving great complexity, frequent variation, rapid changes, unexpected turns of events, and negative cash flow), it is important that they write out a summary page on each of their past investments. How carefully was the investment researched before purchase, how long was it held, the decisive factors that led to a sale, the percentage profit or loss expressed in annualized terms, and performance of the investment following its sale.

A few of these single-page summaries typically will reveal certain patterns such as those already noted: hurried purchases, impulsive sales in the face of temporary adversities, or premature sales when investments finally recover after lengthy holding periods and are on the threshold of large gains.

The particulars of each investment will seem different superficially. For example, one can always think of an excuse, any excuse, to justify a premature sale. However, *although superficial characteristics differ from one investment to another, the basic pattern for each investor usually remains intact.* A rigid person who ignores sound advice until she is forced to sell will do so repeatedly, despite considerable variation from one investment to another.

Not only the hostile, but *all investors should make similar summaries and study them to extract common investment themes or patterns that have led to losses or limited gains.* These patterns should be summarized and written out as brief, general statements to be used as reference and as continued reminders of the circumstances under which investment mistakes are made.

Table 12–1 shows trading patterns which were extracted from transaction summaries of one stock market

Table 12–1 Trading Rules for Avoiding Losses
(Sample Patterns of One Investor)

1. Investor sold stocks prematurely so as to raise cash and purchase another stock that he felt certain would do better.
   RULE: *Do not sell any stock before it makes the move you have anticipated for it just to get into another, seemingly more exciting, situation.*

2. Investor had a tendency to place all his cash into a single stock because, initially, he was convinced it was a fabulous choice. However, he got impatient and sold his single large position so as to purchase something else he felt would make a faster move.
   RULE: *Diversify among five different stocks and stagger your trades—do not buy or sell all five at once.*

3. Investor purchased stocks after exceptional earnings were reported, but failed to make short-term profits.
   RULE: *Remember, in the stock market, hopes are far more important than realized earnings. Purchase on commonly shared great hopes for an issue and sell once the hopes are realized (i.e., profits reported).*

4. Investor had a tendency to make trading decisions while conversing with his broker. Such purchases and sales, made on the spur of the moment, were usually detrimental.
   RULE: *Do not make trading decisions while communicating with your broker. Listen to his recommendation, get off the phone, think about it carefully, and then make a decision.*

(table continues)

Table 12–1 (Continued)

5. Investor sometimes purchased inactive issues because fundamentals indicated these were undervalued. But, being inactive, the issues failed to move fast enough for him. So, he sold to purchase more active issues.

   RULE: *Do not purchase inactive issues, even when you are convinced they are excellent buys.*

6. Investor purchased foreign stocks and did very poorly with such investments because he was unfamiliar with the psychology of these markets and could not time his trades well.

   RULE: *Do not buy foreign stocks.*

7. Investor discussed his stocks with friends, bragging when they did well, and developing a "public commitment" to hold these positions. In this way, he failed to sell and take short-term profits when opportunities arose.

   RULE: *Do not discuss your stock market investments with friends or relatives and do not give stock market advice.*

8. Investor held a stock after extremely positive news. But, the stock declined on very high volume despite the news.

   RULE: *Sell a stock if, after extremely positive news, it declines on unusually high volume.*

---

investor. Each pattern is followed by a trading rule designed to compensate for the temperament-related handicap.

Investors should carefully review their summaries of past transactions and patterns and think out the implications of these *before* they make any trades. In referring to the statements, investors readily will detect how a certain inclination to buy or sell is reminiscent of an established pattern. The recognition will serve as a warning signal and will encourage careful analysis to decide whether any trades are appropriate or necessary at a given time.

Forced self-examination along these lines helps to broaden investors' perspectives by identifying emotional factors which influence purchases and sales. Recognizing emotionally-triggered decisions helps investors to consider other, more realistic, factors. Do the latter call for a purchase or a sale? If not, then it is better to wait for a more opportune time.

In sum, hostile persons, like all others with characteristic investment problems, need to make conscious and explicit their investment patterns and associated faults. They also need to remind themselves repeatedly of these, particularly prior to any investment transaction. If purchase and sale decisions are motivated emotionally, knowledge of the patterns should help them revise those decisions on the basis of more rational investment considerations.

Chapter 13
The Anxious

Steve is a social worker. He was a university student during the Vietnam conflict. Although Steve had an excellent educational background, he was miserable during most of his university career. He worried about the draft, did not enjoy living at home with his parents, and often had doubts about going on in school or what he might do once he graduated.

Like many of his contemporaries, Steve experimented with drugs. Within a short time, he became completely dependent on marijuana. He could not start a day or face problems without first smoking a joint. Once or twice during the school day, particularly prior to anything demanding, he found a secluded spot in which to have another joint. Marijuana had a mellowing effect on Steve. For at least an hour or two, it made him feel more comfortable and less troubled.

Examination periods were especially difficult for Steve. At such times, he slept poorly, was tense, lost his appetite and only snacked on chips or candy, suffered from endless headaches, and became accident-prone. He lost or misplaced his books, his wallet, his keys, and had several car accidents in the course of a two-year period.

The accidents usually were minor, but became of greater concern when he began having problems with his vision. One morning, while driving to school, he felt he could barely see the road. He had been going on for days without sleep and taking strong pain-killers for his headaches almost on an hourly basis. Doctors who examined him did not find any organic basis for the visual problem. So, they prescribed a tranquilizer and recommended rest.

Steve had the same girlfriend during all his college years. She was attractive and sexually promiscuous. She also was self-confident and aggressive and somehow had decided to take charge of Steve. The relationship lasted until the end of their school days when she left him to move to a desert hippie commune. Soon after, just when Steve began working, another equally dominant female filled the place vacated by his ex-girlfriend.

Although Steve now seems to have come a long way from his university days, his temperament remains the same. He still is a worrier and a complainer. A typical sample of his conversation includes descriptions of problems with coworkers or clients, his low salary, his parents' demands on him, or difficulties with his neighbors.

Steve's only significant investment has been a small house he purchased in 1980 at the very end of the real estate boom in California. The mortgage payments required two-thirds of his take-home pay, leaving him barely enough to meet other essential expenses. Steve bought the house expecting to sell it in a year or two with considerable profit. He knew his payments were prohibitive, but was willing to sacrifice for a short while to achieve a large gain. As it turned out, real estate prices declined, he could not sell the house, would not consider giving it up and losing his downpayment, and so lived in great economic difficulty for several years.

GENERAL CHARACTERISTICS OF THE ANXIOUS

Steve has an "anxious" (unpleasant, arousable, submissive) temperament. Such a temperament magnifies and aggravates effects of stress, difficulties, and problems which in themselves induce feelings of displeasure, arousal, and submissiveness. Extremely anxious persons like Steve have very small tolerance for stress and are psychologically maladjusted. In clinical terminology, they are "neurotic."

Being unpleasant, the anxious have negative social expectations which lead them to feel hurt, abused, neglected, or taken advantage of by others. Being arousable, the anxious cannot concentrate sufficiently to maintain balanced views of complex situations. They are drawn to, and focus on, disturbing and troublesome elements which are only peripherally relevant. This lopsided perspective makes it difficult for them to deal adaptively with high uncertainty. Unimportant details distract them. They become forgetful, repeat the same mistakes, and become error- and accident-prone.

Being submissive, the anxious attribute their problems to external causes: situations, circumstances, others, or bad luck. They often turn to friends and relatives for help and are disappointed and hurt when others cannot solve their problems for them.

In the same difficult situation, and in comparison with others, the anxious are more likely to fret, worry, complain, feel uneasy and insecure; be upset, unhappy, dissatisfied; to suffer from insomnia; and to have unresolved difficulties, failures, and coping problems. They also are prone to feel more pain than others and to have a variety of fears or phobias. It is not surprising, then, that the anxious typically avoid exacting or troublesome situations, tending to be drawn to safe, comfortable, and familiar havens.

Importantly, the anxious have little emotional resilience. Negative feelings of concern, discomfort, irritation, frustration, anxiety, fear, or pain generated in one situation last for long periods after they leave it. Indeed, these negative feelings spill over into other unrelated settings or encounters with people, thereby creating difficulties which otherwise would be absent.

Emotional characteristics of the anxious predispose them to psychological dependence on "relaxant" drugs. These drugs are antidotes to anxiety because they increase pleasure, reduce arousal, or increase dominance. Marijuana is one example and when used frequently will increase pleasure and decrease arousal (but will decrease dominance as well). Barbiturates also increase pleasure and decrease arousal. Opiates, such as heroin, increase pleasure and dominance and reduce arousal. When subjected to stress over long periods of time, the anxious may become dependent on such drugs to relieve intolerable anxiety.

Anxious persons generally are apprehensive, or even fearful, of high uncertainty. Being insecure, they are attracted to commercial and social gimmicks which provide a superficial sense of security. They are, thus, easy targets of insurance campaigns or fanatical groups who proselytize and offer simplistic values and lifestyles as all-encompassing solutions to life problems.

INVESTING BY THE ANXIOUS

To understand how the anxious relate to investments, remember that high-uncertainty situations are highly arousing. When high uncertainty is combined with pleasure (e.g., investments doing well), the result is elation; in contrast, when high uncertainty is combined with displeasure, the result is discomfort, distress, anxiety, fear, or panic. High-uncertainty investments, in particular, typically involve difficulties, setbacks, and may require additional infusions of money. These investments, therefore, often generate unpleasant rather than pleasant feelings. This is why uncertainty of investments is proportional to stress (i.e., discomfort, distress, anxiety) levels for investors.

Negative effects of high uncertainty are felt the most by the anxious in comparison with other temperament types. Even a minor difficulty with an investment is likely to be blown out of proportion and to become a psychological drain for the anxious. As a consequence, *in investing as in other areas of life, the insecurity of the anxious translates into a strong desire to be cautious and conservative, to avoid risks, and to find safe and secure havens for their savings.* Thus, the anxious find low-uncertainty investments highly appealing. Savings and money market accounts, Treasury bills, and the like are investments of choice for them.

However, as noted in the following section, the anxious are sometimes seduced to participate in risky investments. Let us say Carla, an anxious type, has been led to buy stocks on margin, borrowing approximately 50 percent of the purchase price. Prices of stocks fluctuate from day-to-day, moving up or down erratically. Sometimes there are gradual upward (or downward) trends over periods of weeks or months, but even these trends are jagged. Assuming that she bought correctly with an upward-moving trend, her emotional reactions during temporary corrections would be critical to success.

Those who succeed at this type of investment have confidence in their stock selections and appraisal of the trend and can take temporary reversals in stride. In contrast, the anxious are emotionally incapable of tolerating adversity, particularly when it is unexpected, rapid, and involves so much complexity that price changes cannot be understood.

This inability to tolerate adversity practically guarantees failure. If stock prices move down for a few consecutive days, the decline seems interminable to Carla. She worries about the investment and loss of her capital. She reads the papers frequently to find reassurance, but is chagrined to find some negative prognoses.

Reading the financial papers is not much help to the anxious because they can always find pro or con expert opinions on any investment. Some writers may disapprove of a particular stock Carla has purchased. Others may suggest the overall downtrend will be long-lasting, while some insist the correction is temporary.

Carla, who turns to external sources (friends, supposed experts, investment newsletters) to allay her fears, inevitably will find information to confirm her worst expectations. Being unpleasant and, therefore, generally pessimistic, she will focus on negative prognostications and overlook positive analyses consistent with her plan. Being arousable, she will be unable to control or limit strong emotions generated by her investment. These will influence and infect most of her daily activities. She will become jittery and minor irritants will take on exaggerated importance. She will lose sleep and rest, feel tired most of the time, become unhappy or morose, and experience the investment as an ever-present burden.

One or two such adverse episodes will suffice to reduce Carla to total defeat. She will break down and sell the stocks prematurely and at a loss just to be rid of the intolerable worry, sleeplessness, misery, and fear.

Carla also would worry if her investment were to do well. Let us say she bought 500 shares of a stock at $42 per share and is fortunate enough to have the price appreciate quickly to $45 per share. Assume also that at $45, the price reverses and begins moving down. She would worry—first, about losing the profit, and when the decline continues, about losing her capital. She would sell at $43 just as the price stabilizes with good potential to resume the uptrend.

CONFORMITY OF THE ANXIOUS: MOB INFLUENCES

The discussion of conformity (Chapter 9) showed that combinations of pleasure, arousal, and submissiveness increase one's susceptibility to social influence. Situations and/or temperaments associated with this feeling make us more willing to do others' bidding, to do favors, to think favorably of advice, to comply with others' wishes, or simply to go along.

The dependent, being pleasant, arousable, and submissive, are thus the most conforming of all temperament types. Anxious persons are arousable and submissive, but unpleasant. They, therefore, become almost as conforming as the dependent, provided the situation is pleasant or when they are with persons they like or respect. In these instances, situationally induced pleasure outweighs temperament-related unpleasantness, resulting in an emotional configuration maximally conducive to conformity.

We already have discussed crowd psychology when prices are high and totally out of proportion to economic reality and when investments seem fail safe. *Of all temperament types, the dependent and the anxious are influenced most by commonly held attitudes of the mob toward investments. And, as with the dependent, conformity of the anxious to the mob traps them into high-uncertainty investments near peaks of investment cycles.*

The anxious, being naturally fearful, avoid risk and moderate- or high-uncertainty investments (whether real-estate, bonds, stocks, or commodities) when these are unpopular, and, therefore, underpriced or reasonably priced. As prices escalate and approach their peaks, the success, fun, and excitement of the crowd produce strong associations of pleasure and arousal to investments. Pressures toward conformity to the mob are, thus, maximized and the anxious who have resisted all along the way finally make the leap.

Since anxious persons are less optimistic than the dependent, they take longer to become convinced of the apparent merits of speculative markets. Compared with the dependent, then, the anxious join the crowd when prices are even higher in booming markets. This almost guarantees their failure, making them even less successful in investing than the dependent.

At other times, the anxious participate in higher-uncertainty investments due to the influence of those they like and respect. A friend or acquaintance may seem to be doing well with a risky investment. Conversations with this person may give the illusion that the investment is simple, provided one follows certain elementary guidelines. The anxious individual also may assume that he can turn to the "expert" for assistance to ensure success. Thus, the idea of financial gain (pleasure) and confidence inspired by someone knowledgeable and successful (dominance) transform anxiety to feelings of vigor and excitement.

As with crowd influence, this effect of a strong mentor or model is equally illusory. In both cases, the anxious invest on the basis of another's knowledge and success and without adequate technical preparation. The misplaced feeling of security slips away easily when the investment does poorly, if the mentor cannot help when things go wrong, or worse yet, when the mentor also suffers losses.

Thus, the initial period of excitement is short-lived. In any investment, prices move down as well as up and, near market tops, nasty and rapid declines are not uncommon. Once money is committed, the anxious quickly discover that there are bad, as well as good, days.

The fragile emotional makeup of the anxious thus leads to losses or only small gains when market conditions are favorable. Typically, because of their inclination to enter markets near their tops, their losses are substantial because price moves are rapid and large in such frothy markets.

The anxious, thus, do poorly with moderate- or high-uncertainty investments because they make investment commitments for the wrong, often emotional, reasons and also because they abandon their strategies for the same reasons. They purchase investments because actions of others generate excitement and a false sense of confidence, not because the investments are timely or make economic sense. They sell promising investments prematurely because of inability to tolerate reversals and inability to maintain perspective on a plan. Alternatively, they hold nonliquid investments through prolonged declines because they are overwhelmed by the prospects of taking substantial short-term losses.

It is also worth noting that, being arousable, the anxious have a tendency to buy on good, and sell on bad, news. Being submissive, they tend to believe in luck and to feel that chance events and others determine success and failure with their investments.

NONLIQUID INVESTMENTS

Some investment vehicles are not as "liquid" (easy to buy or sell) as stocks, bonds, commodities, or financial futures. Examples of nonliquid investments are real estate, precious or semi-precious gems, rare coins, rare stamps, tapestries, carpets, paintings, or other art objects. An investor who buys real estate at a market top may find practically no buyers a few months after the purchase, even if she is willing to take a 15 percent loss. Real estate often takes months to sell and this waiting period costs money in a declining market. Prospective buyers who initially are interested in the discounted property later are discouraged to proceed with the purchase when price erosion continues.

Anxious persons who get involved with nonliquid investments at market tops find that they cannot extricate themselves from the investments in any reasonable way. Like Steve, who bought his house at an exorbitant price and would not face loss of his downpayment but neither could afford the endless, large monthly payments, they find themselves in an investment quagmire. They end up owning properties they do not understand, do not like, and that are constant sources of difficulties and misery.

INVESTMENTS APPROPRIATE FOR THE ANXIOUS

Aside from direct financial losses, participation of the anxious in high-uncertainty investments entails tremendous work-related and psychological costs. Someone who is worried about, and emotionally drained by, her investment cannot attend adequately to her regular work. She suffers from insomnia, becomes less efficient, prone to errors, irritable with coworkers or employees, and generally less effective at work.

With family and friends, she becomes more unpleasant, jittery, easily upset, and generally less fun to be with. Also, she is likely to develop psychosomatic illnesses from the subjectively intolerable pressures of the investment. All in all, the investment has damaging repercussions across a wide range of life situations. Sometimes, costs of these repercussions are far greater than monetary losses from the investments themselves.

When the anxious manage their own investments, they are best off, then, with low-uncertainty investments. These are simple, stable and unchanging, low-risk, and generate positive cash flow. Examples are savings or money market accounts, Treasury bills and notes, and high-safety bonds.

The anxious can take on somewhat higher-uncertainty investments, provided these are managed exclusively by professionals. For instance, they can invest in real estate or the stock and bond markets by purchasing shares in funds that are managed professionally. Being removed from everyday management and decision making reduces uncertainty considerably and to a point where it can be tolerable to the anxious.

As with the dependent, highly popular and speculative investment markets should ring loud warning bells for the anxious. Anxious persons need to be vigilant about their heightened vulnerability to investment fashions. More generally, they need to be aware of their tendency to be drawn to high-uncertainty investments when these seem safe—safety which only is illusory.

If the anxious hold investments in markets which turn popular, a useful guideline is to refrain strictly from increasing the dollar amounts invested. In this way, amounts invested in such markets will be determined under normal circumstances prior to popularity and, therefore, will be dictated by less emotional considerations.

The anxious need not be dismayed by the analysis of problems associated with their temperament. In the long term, investment success depends on gradual and steady accumulation of profits that are reinvested and, therefore, compounded. Participants in high-uncertainty markets may show spectacular short-term gains which they usually gladly disclose to friends and acquaintances. They also may just as easily suffer spectacular losses which they often are reluctant to make public.

So, high-uncertainty investments have an aura of excitement, adventure, and success which grossly is misplaced. Also, such investments usually are a considerable psychological drain for most investors. Few individuals do well steadily at high-uncertainty investing. Those who succeed are well aware of their limitations and have emotional characteristics which permit them to adhere strictly to well-defined investment programs. Those who employ low- or moderate-uncertainty investments may seem like plodders, but oftentimes show better average results than many who invest in livelier markets.

The anxious person who is well aware of his limits and resists temptations to be drawn into inappropriate investments is already ahead of most in the investment game. Increased self-awareness is conducive to a more rational approach to selection of investments or choice of experts to handle one's funds. The steady reinvestment of proceeds from low-risk investments may at times barely keep up with inflation, but nevertheless will help provide the financial security which is most meaningful to the anxious.

Chapter 14
The Disdainful

Wendy is a computer programmer. She is in charge of all computer accounting at a large corporation. Most of Wendy's coworkers do not know much about her, except that she is a brilliant programmer who keeps to herself. They do, however, get the feeling that Wendy chooses not to befriend them.

Wendy is in her mid-thirties and lives alone. Her favorite sports are skiing and tennis where she feels she has a chance to meet affluent, sophisticated men. She prefers relationships to lack intensity and holds her boyfriends at arm's length. Generally, relationships are unsatisfying for Wendy, except for the few that hold her interest during brief periods. She basically is a loner and treats her companions as playthings that she discards when she tires of them.

Wendy is very well off. When people get nosy about this, she hints vaguely about some inheritance. Actually, Wendy has made all the money herself. A few years ago, she was dating the chief executive officer of a medium-sized corporation. He flew her places in his corporate jet, took her overseas sometimes, dined at some of the best restaurants, and stayed at the finest hotels. Wendy liked all that, but these benefits hardly compared with the fantastic opportunity he unwittingly dropped in her lap.

One evening, they drove out of town to a beautiful country inn where they had dinner, consuming two bottles of wine in the process. Back in their room, her companion seemed particularly expansive and reckless. He presented her with a beautiful necklace and, when she protested, said something to the effect that he easily could afford it since he soon would get a huge windfall. During the ensuing two hours, he revealed, after impressing Wendy that she should treat the information with the strictest of confidence, that his company was about to be acquired. His company stock which at the time was selling around $16 per share was to be purchased at $32 per share. Wendy took in the information quietly, congratulated her friend, and dropped the topic as though it were of passing interest.

For the next several weeks, she curtailed most of her social activities and worked intently to devise a scheme to profit from this precious information. She needed a large amount of capital very soon and only had $35,000 in savings. There was no way she could legitimately borrow the kind of money she needed. So, her plan involved a temporary "loan" from her employer.

The following is only an outline of her intricate plan. She opened accounts at various banks using names of several bogus businesses. These businesses billed her employer for services and products. Wendy arranged for the bills to be paid through her computer system, bypassing routine checks. The bills were small and would not be noticed in any casual inspection—they totaled approximately one million dollars.

Wendy's next step was to transfer these funds from the bogus company accounts to her Swiss bank account which she had opened on one of her previous trips to Europe. The stock she needed to purchase was listed on the New York Stock Exchange and was traded actively. She instructed her Geneva bank to purchase 115,000 shares for her account at prices ranging from $16 to $17 per share. The purchases were made on 50 percent margin, with the bank lending her half the purchase price.

Two months after these stock purchases, the buyout was announced in the press and the shares shot up to $29. Wendy immediately instructed her bank to sell the stock in 5,000 share blocks at prices above $29 per share. Net proceeds in excess of $3.3 million were realized from these sales. After paying off the borrowed funds plus interest, she was left with $2.3 million in her Swiss account.

Although the payments from her employer to the bogus businesses were planned carefully, Wendy knew these would not stand up to scrutiny. So, at this point, she returned all funds she had received from the bogus companies back to their accounts. Next, each of those businesses in turn refunded the sums they had billed her employer. Once the exact amounts she had paid out for nonexistent services and products were back in place, she obliterated all computer records of bills, payments to the bogus companies, and refunds. There was no trace at her corporation of the temporary absence of funds. The only traces left were at local banks which had records of the bogus transactions. But, there was little chance of anyone from her company looking into those when everything on the home front was in proper order.

As it turned out, the buyout did not materialize. The buyers decided to lower their offer and the new, lower offer was rejected. The stock dropped back to $15 per share and the entire sequence of events went down in financial records as another failed merger attempt.

GENERAL CHARACTERISTICS OF THE DISDAINFUL

Wendy epitomizes the disdainful (unpleasant, unarousable, dominant) temperament. She is contemptuous of most people. Disdainful persons like Wendy are loners and do not have warm or loving relationships. They are selfish, aloof, and cold and are not moved easily by the or grief of others. They are preoccupied with themselves and are uncaring, uninvolved, and uninterested in others or in the world about them. They keep to themselves and get involved with others when it is to their benefit. Narcissists typically are disdainful, but occasionally may have hostile temperaments.

Disdainful persons handle emotionally difficult situations calmly and with deliberation. Being unarousable, they cope with detachment, calm, and panache in stressful situations which ordinarily would overwhelm the arousable. Being dominant, they are self-confident and disciplined and know they can deal independently and successfully with problems.

The disdainful are defensive like the hostile. However, being less arousable than the hostile, they are not as quick to infer negative insinuations, insult, rejection, or harmful intent. Also, unlike the hostile, they do not respond impulsively, openly, or violently to troublesome others or situations. Instead, they react calmly and carefully, waiting for opportunities to redress the balance. They also are less eager than the hostile to change others or society at large. For the disdainful, such concerns are wasteful and futile.

As much as the disdainful are unfeeling and callous about others, they are equally hard-driving and self-disciplined when they set out to achieve their own goals. They lack scruples and can be devious, calculating, and Machiavellian, though typically nonviolent, in striving toward those goals.

For the disdainful, work or investments constitute opportunities to outperform and even humiliate others. Seeing others do poorly simply reinforces their generalized contempt for people. It does not bother them when, in the process of achieving their own goals, others are shortchanged or hurt. This is how the disdainful, more than any other temperament type, make up the ranks of professional, nonviolent criminals.

"Sociopaths" and "psychopaths" have the temperament characteristics of the hostile or the disdainful, but
are classified as one group in traditional psychiatric terminology. Our typology makes the critical distinction on
arousability lacking in the traditional nomenclature. It
thus permits us to distinguish the violent and impulsive
from the deliberate and calculating among those diag-
nosed as sociopaths or psychopaths.

INVESTING BY THE DISDAINFUL

The disdainful, like Wendy, and Donald in "Cases," tend
to view investments as contests—their gains being others'
losses. Investment success is highly reinforcing to them
in that it confirms their sense of self-worth and superiority.

Ability of the disdainful to remain calm, appraising,
and detached in highly emotional circumstances associated with high-uncertainty investments permits them to
consider their options rationally. Their dominance allows
them to pursue their strategies with determination. The
disdainful are thus highly successful in investing and are
excelled only by the relaxed who have the ideal temperament in this area.

Investing, as we have seen, is a two-stage process:
preparation before money is committed and investment
management after such commitment. Being unarousable
and dominant, the disdainful are hardly impulsive or
blindly conforming when they prepare to invest. Since
they do not have much respect for people anyway, they
gravitate to more abstract and factual sources of information during the preparatory stage. They study various
investment strategies before deciding on methods best
suited to themselves.

Such preparation enhances confidence and their
ability to follow through on a particular strategy once
money is committed. They, thus, maintain a long-term,

broad perspective even when temporary circumstances are adverse and their investments do poorly.

The disdainful, like the relaxed, deal with their investments in a detached and unemotional manner. If they invest in the fast-paced stock or futures markets, they probably have a set schedule of preparation and planning during hours when markets are closed. They update information necessary to track their investments and make trading decisions at leisure, balancing the pros and cons for each trade. Such background work done when markets are closed and emotional pressures are attenuated are important contributors to success.

As with the relaxed, the disdainful also do not hesitate to close out loss-prone positions and to move on to other, more profitable, trades. They easily overcome negative feelings caused by investment losses and do not brood over these or let them influence their work or social lives.

The archetypal disdainful investor is one who invests independently and devotes daily attention and effort to his investments. He does not consult with others, is generally contemptuous of the financial news media, and considers most of this product to be *post facto* explanation or commentary or, worse yet, to be a confusing jumble of noise.

The disdainful investor waits and buys after a lengthy decline and only after continuing losses of many have driven most others from the investment, generated a negative popular aura about it, and thereby created unusual bargains.

The disdainful person sells when his waiter, barber, shoe-shine boy, and mother-in-law wax enthusiastic about a particular investment and even start to buy despite their meager resources. The disdainful derive great pleasure from being proven right in going against the
̶ ͏̶ at both the bottom and at the top of cyclical price
Their temperament is suited for calm, detached,

and calculated antagonism—moving against others with deliberation comes naturally.

Lest the reader be misled to think that the disdainful always succeed in investing, we should note that everybody, including the disdainful, can make mistakes. The disdainful make fewer mistakes, however, because, unlike the dependent or the anxious, they make their moves independently of the crowd. Also, unlike the hostile, the disdainful do not get overly emotional about investments and can deal with these rationally, patiently, and in accordance with a planned strategy of action.

How is it that the relaxed do even better than the disdainful in investing? The relaxed are more pleasant and it is easier for them to tolerate, and cope with, unpleasant events associated with investments. The relaxed relate well to people and can work along with others to accomplish their investment goals. Therefore, more investment options are open to the relaxed than to the disdainful who typically restrict themselves to investments where they do not need cooperation from others.

Overall, both the relaxed and the disdainful are calm, patient, and pursue their goals with confidence and determination. The relaxed, however, can employ more difficult, annoying, and irritating investment strategies which have greater payoffs. For instance, compared with the disdainful, relaxed persons are better equipped to form partnerships and to use others' funds for investing, paying themselves significant percentages of the profits as management fees. In comparison, disdainful persons would much rather work alone and usually lack the interpersonal skills to handle complications which arise in working closely with others. Thus, the disdainful are less able to use financial resources of others to generate profits for themselves.

Relaxed persons also have the potential to build great financial empires because they can work with others, can lead effectively, and delegate responsibility when competent help is available. The efforts of many working together easily can surpass those of a single individual who must work alone. And, the disdainful usually work alone because they do not like others, have difficulty getting along, and in any case are generally mistrustful and do not care to reveal their investment strategy to subordinates. The disdainful, then, have a more limited potential to amass great wealth through investments that involve the cooperation of many.

Chapter 15
The Bored

June is a clothing designer in her mid-forties. About fifteen years ago, her family provided financial backing so she could manufacture her designs. She and her uncle, who organized and ran the business, manufactured a small line of high-fashion sports- and leisure-wear. The designs were received extremely well and their business expanded rapidly. Three years ago, their company was purchased by a large conglomerate for $42 million. June's share of the net proceeds after taxes was $13 million in cash.

June has two college-age children who are away at school. She was divorced during the up-beat and hectic period when her business was growing in leaps and bounds. Life has been drastically different for her ever since the buyout. She travels almost all the time, spending a few weeks in each area she visits. She travels alone and does a lot of shopping.

Even though this sounds like a marvelous success story, June actually has not been very happy ever since the sale of her business. Her traveling is a frivolous search for excitement and an escape from an undercurrent of boredom and loneliness which become intolerable when she stays home. Twelve years of active design work in a rapid-growth business skillfully managed by her uncle had kept her intensely occupied and helped her compensate for her bored temperament. Now, however, she does not have any equivalent complex and demanding stimulus; she also does not have her children or a husband at home. Having to live alone without external demands on her time has unmasked her mild temperament-related problem.

Like many of the bored, June uses fantasy and unrealistic goals as an escape. Each visit to a new part of the world is preceded by exaggerated hopes and daydreams about the sites and the people she will encounter. She fantasizes at length about an African safari, a boat trip down the Amazon, or a sailing trip along the Adriatic coast.

When she actually embarks on such a journey, the first few days feel all right, but she rapidly tires of the routines, the discomforts, and her fellow travelers whom she easily typecasts. Although there is an initial element of novelty and excitement, daily patterns and routines of travel reduce the arousing quality of her new surroundings and she loses interest in the "adventure." She becomes disappointed, bored, socially withdrawn, and spends hours each day reading novels. Without a close companion to help her along, she simply does not have the drive to make something worthwhile and fulfilling out of her trips and the many people she meets.

June has taken a similar carefree and superficial tack toward her recent investments. Without much investigation or study, she has invested hundreds of thousands in a small gold-mining operation, a couple of feature films, a Broadway show, a horse-breeding ranch, and a resort hotel. Promoters of these projects found June to be an easy target of their fanciful tales of tax advantages and potential large returns. To date, June has failed to reap any profits from these investments. Fortunately, thanks to the insistent advice of her uncle and business partner, the bulk of her cash is invested in various money-market accounts.

June's problem with investing, as with her travels, is her frivolous approach. She does not research her investments, readily accepts the rosy pictures painted by promoters, and commits money because she needs to believe each project will be a success. She enjoys the fantasies she has about each investment: the people she will meet, the successful outcomes, and her own role as an influential participant.

A more debilitating case of bored temperament is illustrated by Alex, a high-school art teacher. Alex also is a painter and has little enthusiasm for his teaching; it is his meal ticket. His career aspirations relate primarily to painting.

Alex's efforts at painting are erratic because he is discouraged easily. When he does manage to muster enough drive to work on a series of new ideas, his hopes keep him going for a few weeks. But, when he is turned down by a gallery or when others are critical of his work, he is shattered, gets depressed, and gives up painting for weeks.

Since Alex is single and lives alone, his depressive periods are extremely painful. At such times, he feels hopeless and believes his efforts at painting are futile. He gets home from school drained and barely able to warm up a bowl of soup. He falls asleep on his couch, wakes up two or three hours later feeling lethargic and bored, without the strength to do anything about it. He has so little energy, he cannot even take a shower and get into some clean clothes, call a friend, go for a walk, go to a movie or restaurant, or plan a date.

He spends these evenings snacking on junk foods, drinking scotch whiskey, and watching television. He does not enjoy the shows he watches and frequently switches programs mid-stream. He goes to bed disgusted with himself, unhappy about his social isolation, and despairing of his art.

Alex invests his savings in the stock market, buying low-priced issues or "odd lots" (less than 100 shares) of more expensive stocks. He bases his purchase decisions on reports in the financial papers. Anytime he reads a promising story about a company, he is tempted to buy its shares. The greater the expectations of quick gain, the more likely he is to act on the information and sell what he owns to make the new purchase. This undisciplined and poorly-informed trading style has led to steady losses over the years, robbing Alex of opportunities to use his savings to cheer up his life with more recreation, dating, or travel.

GENERAL CHARACTERISTICS OF THE BORED

Like June, Alex has a "bored" (unpleasant, unarousable, submissive) temperament. June represents a mild case of bored temperament that is strongly aggravated by the large and discontinuous change in her life situation. Alex, on the other hand, has a more serious temperament problem.

In more extreme cases, the bored are withdrawn socially and spend much time alone, engaged in solitary activities. They tend to sleep long hours without feeling refreshed. They have difficulty leaving the bed because they do not have the energy or enthusiasm to initiate a social or physical activity, let alone the stamina to take on new problems or difficult tasks. They feel helpless or impotent to deal with their life situations or problems and sometimes barely manage to hold on to their jobs. They are inattentive to their clothing and physical appearance. They seem unkempt and unattractive, or even bizarre, because of failure to wash, attend to hair or makeup, or change into clean clothing.

In these more extreme cases of boredom, it feels like being stuck in low gear. There is much inertia in the slow and monotonous pace. It is difficult to shift from the physical inactivity and mental dullness of low arousal to the high arousal entailed in calling a friend, doing some household chores, or going out for a walk. Visiting friends or taking on new work become formidable tasks. All these require an increase in arousal, a gearing-up in physical activity and mental alertness, which feels burdensome, discontinuous, and out of reach. The bored, thus, continue on feeling unhappy and depressed, preoccupied with imaginary physical ailments, and unable to make the effort to improve their circumstances.

When alone, the bored feel aimless and hopeless. For stimulation, they seek activities that require little effort. This is how they often are tempted to overeat, use alcohol to excess, or use stimulant drugs. Eating, drinking, drugs, television, and, in some cases, indiscriminate sex are the favorite pastimes of the bored. These activities provide temporary relief from endless hours of emptiness and inactivity.

INVESTING BY THE BORED

For persons like June, Alex, and Roger in "Cases," investments need to be easy and must provide quick and easy relief from despair. The bored do not have the energy or stamina to study and investigate an investment field or to plan with the long-range view in sight. Instead, they are drawn to simple, pat formulas which seem effortless and highly promising.

Minimal preparation, superficial knowledge, and reliance on high-pressure sales pitches usually leads the bored to poor investment choices. As is characteristic of all submissive individuals who are poorly prepared and must rely on opinions of others, the bored lack confidence in their investments. So, when their investments do poorly or fail to produce the rapid gains expected, they are discouraged, sell, and move on.

Since the bored require frequent good news and pleasant stimulation, few of their investments live up to expectations. They sell investments prematurely, even if these may be promising, and cast around for substitutes.

And, at any given time, there is no dearth of far-fetched investment schemes touted as the next source of great rewards. Thus, the bored are drawn from one dubious investment scheme to another, casting at random and without much thought, hoping for a big break. Typically, then, investments of the bored lack a consistent strategy. Instead, their trading is an impulsive and frivolous search for quick gains.

Hopes and fantasies relating to upcoming, yet untried, investments provide emotional relief to the bored—relief from loneliness, inactivity, and helplessness. Alas, once an investment is made, reality turns out to be bleak compared with expectation and it becomes necessary to move on to other investments to satisfy the psychological craving.

Some forms of investing, particularly speculation, are at times compared with gambling. Indeed, when one approaches investments whimsically, without discipline, and with unrealistic hopes for quick, easy gains, the underlying psychological process is similar to that associated with gambling.

Among all temperament types, the bored are most likely to share a gambler's mentality and emotional needs. Paradoxically, the exuberant, who are exactly the opposite of the bored, are second in line to the bored in approaching investments in a gambler's way. Whereas the bored seek investments frivolously to gain emotional relief, the exuberant do so because it fits their general style.

Considering their emotional vulnerabilities, it is crucial that the bored let seasoned professionals manage their investments. Recommendations made to the submissive (Chapter 6) are applicable here as well. Low-uncertainty money-market, corporate-bond, or municipal-bond funds may be dull, but provide steady returns. Financial gains from such conservative investments (plus savings from avoided investment losses) should allow the bored to compensate for the dullness of their investments by spicing up other areas of their lives.

Chapter 16

Life Circumstances

Life circumstances refer to our social and work situations. A daily two-hour round trip commute to work is a significant life circumstance, as is absence from home necessitated by frequent work-related air travel. Marriage to a neurotic person or to an alcoholic is a life circumstance and so is great wealth.

Other examples of life circumstances are responsibility for the care of one or two (or a dozen) children; work which is all-consuming and mentally and physically draining and work which is comfortable and fun; a mate who is an economic asset and one who is a liability; a mate who is a psychological asset and a resource to solve everyday life problems and one who is a psychological liability, generating problems and complicating existing ones.

Major alterations in our lives are also life circumstances. Some examples are marriage, birth of a child, assumption of a large financial obligation such as a home mortgage, death of a spouse or of a close relative, loss of work and extended unemployment, divorce, an extramarital affair which impacts on marriage, children moving away from home, promotion at work, a large inheritance, falling in love, business problems which necessitate layoffs of long-time coworkers and employees, getting involved in a prolonged and difficult lawsuit, developing a chronic physical ailment, or severe injury.

Life circumstances are in part a result of one's temperament. Only certain kinds of people are willing to spend many hours each week to commute to work. Again, specific emotional characteristics lead to selecting a neurotic mate, having a very large family, keeping an all-consuming job, allowing work-related travel to keep one away from home, overextending oneself financially with burdensome debts, having frequent accidents, or experiencing marital difficulties.

Nevertheless, it also is important to recognize that we do not and cannot control all our life situations. Others and events beyond our control also shape our everyday environments and activities. So, it is useful to be able to describe the aggregate influence of these life circumstances and to distinguish this combined influence from the effects of temperament.

For our purposes, life circumstances are described in terms of their emotional effects. Are they pleasant or unpleasant, arousing or unarousing, dominance- or submissiveness-inducing? A large mortgage debt makes one feel displeasure, arousal, and submissiveness. This feeling of discomfort or distress recurs on and off as long as the debt is a significant part of one's finances. An all-consuming job which leaves one exhausted and drained at the end of the work day generates feelings of displeasure, low arousal, and submissiveness during evenings after work, even though the work itself involves high arousal. In fact, it is continued high arousal during work (just like the high arousal during exercise) that results in exhaustion and accompanying low arousal afterwards.

As with temperament, we use eight major constellations of emotion states to characterize life circumstances.

CIRCUMSTANCES THAT MAKE PEOPLE EXUBERANT

We refer to the combination of pleasure, arousal, and dominance as "exuberance." Various shades of this constellation are described as "bold," "creative," "vigorous," "powerful," or "admired." Life situations that result in exuberant feelings are: a happy and stimulating home and recreational life; fulfilled hopes and aspirations; trouble-free and exciting companionship; physical health and vigor associated with a regular program of strenuous physical exercise; or success at work with a challenging job.

Major changes in one's life situation also can bring on exuberant feelings. Some examples are promotion at work, a new job that presents many opportunities for self-improvement and advancement, election to an important office, move to a better residence, engagement or marriage, a highly desired childbirth, or a large inheritance.

Our analysis of the investment style of exuberant persons (Chapter 8) applies equally to individuals whose life situations are conducive to exuberance. We first will consider the sole contribution of life circumstances to investment decisions and actions. Later, we will see how temperament characteristics moderate the impact of life circumstances and must be averaged in for a correct, overall picture.

As with the exuberant, persons whose life situations make them feel exuberant will tend to be active, take risks, feel in charge, be reckless, be impulsive, and have fun. When situations create feelings of exuberance, it is tempting to treat investments as playthings requiring little effort, patience, or discipline. Such an attitude, however, is more suited to gambling than to investing and can result in losses.

Investors who are caught up in exuberant circumstances need to rein in optimism and reflex-like attraction to exciting, varied, risky and fun investments. They should recognize that their life situations limit their abilities to handle moderate- and high-uncertainty investments. If they invest for themselves, they require cautious planning and commitment to low-uncertainty investments.

Basically, investments ought to take a back seat to work and social activities for those whose life situations lead to exuberance. They should concentrate on things they do well and where they have a clear record of success. If they insist on greater returns from investments, they can rely on professionally managed programs of moderate uncertainty, thus "borrowing" the necessary discipline and emotional distance.

CONDITIONS THAT MAKE PEOPLE BORED

The combination of displeasure, low arousal, and submissiveness defines the feeling of being "bored." Some variants are feeling "depressed," "dejected," "hopeless," "lonely," "sad," "tired," or "exhausted." Conditions at work or at home that induce boredom are permeated with routine, slow pace, monotony; lack the possibility of change, improvement, hope, and success; or entail an outlook that is bleak, despairing, or expectant of failure.

Specific examples are retirement and accompanying inactivity; living alone and socially isolated; a career that feels like a treadmill; manual, monotonous labor in the same situation year after year; or a family situation that feels like a trap and is unsatisfying, demoralizing, and bland.

Paradoxically, boredom arises either from monotony, lack of challenge, or lack of hope, or alternatively, from highly stressful situations that last for periods of months or years and involve too much change and conflict, or overwhelming, recurrent, and unavoidable problems. Examples are insurmountable economic hardships, familial problems, job-related conflicts and difficulties, or chronic, painful ailments. Long lasting stress eventually drains the physical organism of its ability to fight back. Literally exhausted, the organism is incapable of mounting sufficient arousal to sustain any efforts to combat the problems.

Boredom, whether associated with temperament or caused by life circumstances, has similar effects on investing. The bored seek investments that are easy and provide relief from pain and unhappiness. Like the exuberant, they approach investments with a gambler's frivolous attitude. They do not have the energy or stamina to study and investigate and are drawn to effortless investments that promise exaggerated gains.

Boring life circumstances, thus, lead to flighty and self-indulgent investment attitudes that lack discipline, confidence, and long-range planning. Individuals in these situations have an unrealistic need for pleasant stimulation from investments. However, few investments provide this without also being discouraging, slow-paced, or resulting in losses from time to time.

Poor preparation and superficial and unrealistic expectations quickly lead to discouragement with investments when these do not meet expectations or when they temporarily do poorly. The bored give up and sell such investments, taking losses and moving on to other, superficially more promising ones.

Given these emotional constraints, those who have boring life circumstances are best off having professionals manage their savings in low- to moderate-uncertainty investments. They can have some stimulation from periodic comparisons of their investments in various funds or by shifting parts of their assets to newly discovered funds with superior recent records. Their investments, managed professionally and at an emotional distance, will limit losses and occasionally provide gains and excitement.

SITUATIONS THAT MAKE PEOPLE DEPENDENT

We refer to the combination of pleasure, arousal, and submissiveness as feeling "dependent." "Amazed," "in-

fatuated," "surprised," "impressed," "loved," and "fascinated" describe various shades of this constellation.
Those who are guided by outside forces at home or at
work and have varied, exciting lives tend to have such
feelings.

One example is the stimulating mate who takes
charge and creates an interesting life at home. The ben-
eficiary willingly goes along because the mate does so
well organizing things. Other examples are an older sib-
ling or relative taking charge and guiding a young person
in his social life or work; a subservient partner deriving
benefits from work companions who are creative, adventuresome, and excel at their jobs; or a lengthy appren-
ticeship that is both educational and fun.

Life circumstances and changes that are conducive
to dependency lead one to become submissive, to follow
rather than to lead, and to let others pave the way, give
direction, or organize activities. It becomes easier to take
on attitudes, opinions, and values of those one likes,
trusts, and respects.

As in the case of those with dependent temperaments, persons with life situations conducive to dependency rely on others when they have difficulties, failures,
illnesses, pains, or anxieties. They tend to lose the initiative for independent action and turn to others for ideas
and reassurance to proceed with projects they initiate.

Our discussion of investing by dependent persons,
their investment pitfalls, and methods to overcome de-
pendency-related handicaps also applies to those whose
life circumstances engender dependency.

When someone has a life situation conducive to
dependency, but has a different, for instance anxious,
temperament, we average the separate emotional effects
of temperament and life situation to understand their
investment style. The averaging yields investment characteristics of both the anxious and the dependent. For
this example, the result is very high arousal and submissiveness together with neutral pleasantness. A person

with this temperament and situation combination would do well to strongly avoid high-uncertainty investments. Chapter 18 contains detailed examples of this averaging process.

CIRCUMSTANCES THAT MAKE PEOPLE DISDAINFUL

The combination of displeasure, low arousal, and dominance defines feeling "disdainful." Other terms used to describe variants of this emotion are "uninterested," "uncaring," "unconcerned," "aloof," "blasé," or "selfish."

Life situations sometimes make it possible for a person to be self-indulgent, selfish, withdrawn, and unemotional. Generally, these are work or social situations that encourage callous and unemotional mistreatment of others. One instance is solitary work in antagonistic, but distant, relationships to others. A Western technician who is paid exorbitantly high wages to work in an oil-rich nation may be isolated socially, bored, uninterested, and feel superior to his hosts.

Situations which create feelings of disdain lead to investment behaviors similar to those of disdainful persons. To infer overall investment style, we average the emotional impact of life situation with the effect of temperament.

CONDITIONS THAT MAKE PEOPLE RELAXED

The combination of pleasure, low arousal, and dominance is described as "relaxed." Other shades of this feeling are "comfortable," "leisurely," "unperturbed," "untroubled," or "secure."

Life situations associated with these feelings are stress- free, slow-paced, pleasant, and enhance feelings of control and influence over one's affairs. An attractive, harmonious, predictable, and patterned home or work situation which one can guide in the desired direction is conducive to relaxation.

An important aspect of a person's life circumstance is his experience with, or expertise in, a specific investment field. Some people select careers in the investment world. Others, though not professionally involved, may nevertheless accumulate considerable expertise over a period of years of investing in stocks, commodities, or financial instruments.

Irrespective of temperament, accumulated knowledge and expertise through experience in an investment area increase one's dominance and reduce one's arousal when dealing with those investments.

Of these two emotional effects of experience, dominance is the strongest. The experienced person feels more in control, confident, and in charge of his investment. The second effect, low arousal, results because experience and knowledge provide many opportunities to discover patterns and, thereby, to reduce complexity and unexpected quality of events while investing. The same investment, thus, has most uncertainty for the novice, less for the moderately experienced investor, and least uncertainty for the expert.

Expertise with an investment area, then, creates two important ingredients of relaxation—dominance and low arousal. And, relaxation, whether generated by expertise or by other life circumstances, produces investment behaviors similar to those of relaxed persons. Therefore, relaxing life circumstances enhance investment success.

Generally, to assess a person's investment style, we consider both his life circumstances and his temperament. When a relaxing life situation is combined with any temperament (for example, an anxious one) we average effects of the situation with those of temperament to arrive at the resulting investment style. For the combination cited, benefits of a relaxing situation are canceled by drawbacks of an anxious temperament, resulting in an average or nondistinctive investment style.

CIRCUMSTANCES THAT MAKE PEOPLE ANXIOUS

"Anxious" is the term used to describe the combination of displeasure, arousal, and submissiveness. Variants are feeling "pained," "unsafe," "embarrassed," "uncomfortable," or "humiliated."

Home and work situations which bring on this cluster of feelings are problem-ridden, involve frequent failures and conflicts, and generally are stressful. Some examples are marital conflict and divorce, loss of a spouse or of a close and loved relative, troubles at work, loss of a job, involvement in lengthy legal conflicts, or burdensome financial obligations.

Situations conducive to anxiety lead to an investment style similar to that of persons with anxious temperaments. Thus, the style, problems, and limitations noted for those with anxious temperaments apply equally to those who have anxiety-producing life situations.

Consider a dependent person in a stressful life situation. When we average the separate effects of his life situation and temperament, it becomes clear that he will be unsuccessful with investments of even moderate uncertainty.

SITUATIONS THAT MAKE PEOPLE DOCILE

"Docile" is the term used to define the combination of pleasure, low arousal, and submissiveness. Other shades of this constellation are "sheltered," "protected," "tranquilized," "consoled," or "quiet."

Life situations associated with these feelings are pleasant, stress-free, slow-paced, patterned, and predictable. A quiet, comfortable, and regular home or work life—where others are in charge, provide economic security, and resolve problems—is conducive to feeling docile. The investment style of someone in such a situation resembles that described for those with docile temperaments.

Combined temperament and situation effects, for instance, for someone with a bored temperament in a situation conducive to docile feelings would result in an emotional base with average chances of success at investing.

CONDITIONS THAT MAKE PEOPLE HOSTILE

The combination of displeasure, arousal, and dominance is described as "hostile." Variants of this feeling are feeling "cruel," "hateful," "scornful," "angry," and "disgusted."

Work and home situations that are full of changes, unpredictable events, unpleasant surprises, and where one has a position of responsibility result in hostile feelings. Some examples are a leader making decisions that have lasting adverse effects on others, a supervisor laying off long-term employees, or parents having problems with children who misbehave.

Life circumstances that create hostile feelings result in an investment style similar to that of persons with hostile temperaments. Thus, our discussion of investing by the hostile applies also to persons whose life situations result in long-lasting periods of hostility.

CHANGES IN LIFE CIRCUMSTANCES OVER TIME

Consideration of life circumstances has important implications for investments of the same person over time.

Most of us go through different stages in our lives. One stage lasting a few years may be reasonably stable, comfortable, and tranquil, with low activity at home and at work. Another stage could involve major shifts and rapid change requiring significant readjustments: closely-spaced births of offspring, rapid advancement at work, or periods fraught with interpersonal, economic, or career-related hardships.

It helps to be sensitive to the emotional climate created by life circumstances and the effects this has on investments. Being aware of significant emotional shifts created by the environment, we can modify our investment styles and goals to make them more compatible with our life situations. Specifically, someone who invests in stocks with moderate success could increase her involvement in the stock market during tranquil and stress-free periods. She might monitor her trades more closely and possibly experiment with alternative and more ambitious trading techniques. On the other hand, during more stressful periods, she might reduce active participation in the stock market, simply purchase shares in a mutual fund, and thereby, drastically reduce uncertainty.

Even in the case of someone who holds the same job over a period of many years, there can be significant variations in job-related stress over time. Periods of high stress involving new projects and people, large-scale changes, upheaval, and continued demands would be combined with investments in low-uncertainty instruments. In contrast, periods of low stress with few changes at work, no new assignments or projects, and generally routine procedures and work practices could be combined with higher-uncertainty investments.

WEALTH

Wealth and the lack of it are important aspects of one's life condition and require separate consideration. The psychological impact of wealth varies, depending on how it is acquired and the speed with which it increases or decreases.

Roughly, there are two states of wealth. In one state, the individual is used to wealth, having inherited it perhaps, does not have to work hard to maintain it, and almost takes it for granted. This is a comfortable and relaxed state of wealth and its emotional components are pleasure, low arousal, and dominance. The opposite of this is lack of sufficient financial resources and accompanying discomfort and anxiety.

Comfortable wealth, insofar as it is conducive to relaxed feelings, creates a psychological advantage in investing. In contrast, lack of wealth and a chronic shortage of sufficient investment funds induce discomfort and tension, and thereby constitute a definite psychological handicap in investing.

A second kind of wealth involves continuous struggle. In this more common form of wealth, the individual works hard to maintain or enhance his financial position. Thus, the accompanying feelings involve high arousal, and may also involve displeasure. So, the emotional impact of this life condition is generally harmful to investing.

We also should consider cases where there is a sudden increase in wealth. Examples are actors who suddenly get a big break in the movies, musicians who have their first big hit, young athletes who are awarded multi-million dollar contracts, individuals who inherit large sums, or those who win lotteries. This kind of life change is exhilarating and is conducive to feelings of exuberance. As we have seen, situations that make people exuberant constitute a definite handicap in investing.

Finally, we need to consider sudden losses of wealth. Examples are loss of a very lucrative job, major investment-related losses, or loss of a spouse who was the source of substantial income. The short-term reaction to such changes is displeasure, heightened arousal, and submissiveness. This combination is anxiety and presents the greatest handicap to investors. The long-term reaction to loss of wealth could be depression (or boredom) and this, again, is a deterrent to success in high-uncertainty investing.

In short, to understand the impact of wealth (or lack of wealth) on investment success, we first must analyze the specific circumstances of wealth and decide on their emotional impact. This should be an easy matter if you are judging your own situation or that of someone you know well. You would pinpoint the pleasure, arousal, and dominance levels associated with wealth or lack of it and would describe the combination in terms of a single emotion term (e.g., relaxed). Next, you could refer to the corresponding section above to see how the particular condition affects investing.

SUMMARY

The framework presented permits the use of analogous concepts to analyze the emotional tone of temperament and emotions created by life circumstances. Generally, it should be easy enough to scrutinize one's life situation and decide whether it is pleasant or unpleasant, arousing or unarousing, and whether it makes one feel dominant or submissive. Once these three judgments are made, we can pinpoint the emotional impact of our life situation to one of the eight basic emotion categories discussed above. Having done so, we easily can evaluate whether our life circumstances are a help or a hindrance to high-uncertainty investing.

We have noted that one's life circumstances are in part a function of one's temperament. Thus, it is common that a dependent person becomes enmeshed in a situation engendering dependency or that a relaxed one creates a relaxing life situation for herself. Such overlap presents no difficulties from the standpoint of our analysis. When we discover that temperament and life circumstances coincide and mutually reinforce one another, the averaging of the two sources simply confirms the influence of either and reminds us of the more pervasive influence of temperament.

On the other hand, separate consideration of life circumstances also allows us to become aware of external and chance influences that create an emotional impact differing from that of a person's temperament. In such cases, the two-pronged approach gives us an opportunity to consider discrepant influences of life circumstances and to average them into the separate effects of temperament. This combined emotional impact from both sources serves as a summary guideline for understanding investment behaviors.

Chapter 17

A Program of Self-Assessment

By now, you probably have arrived at certain conclusions about your own temperament, the emotional impact of your life situation, and some of the common patterns in your investment style. This chapter contains specific guidelines you need to make such evaluations and should help you improve the tentative assessments you have made up to this point.

SELF-ASSESSMENT OF TEMPERAMENT

As we have seen, temperament is described completely in terms of three basic dimensions. To assess anyone's temperament, we need to know whether they are pleasant or unpleasant, arousable or unarousable, and dominant or submissive.

Pleasantness

Three important criteria pinpoint the pleasant-unpleasant aspect of temperament. These are positive versus negative social expectations, general optimism versus pessimism, and pleasant versus unpleasant topics of conversation.

You need to examine yourself in terms of these three criteria. Do you expect your contacts with people you socialize and work with or your encounters with strangers to be fun, rewarding, and satisfying? Or, do you expect such social contacts to be uncomfortable, unsatisfying, distressing, or even painful or punishing? Do you act according to positive expectations and draw out positive reactions from companions and even strangers—reactions that reinforce your positive expectations? Or, do you act according to negative expectations, being reserved, withdrawn, uncomfortable, defensive, or even openly negative with, or antagonistic to, others.

Remember also that those who have positive expectations tend to have many friends, spend the bulk of their free time with people in various social and recreational situations. In contrast, people with negative expectations have fewer friends and spend most of their leisure time in solitary activities such as reading, watching television, doing individual sports, or busy with hobbies.

Positive social expectations are part of a broader pattern of expectations about life in general, or *optimism*—viewing life in a positive and hopeful light, expecting most things to turn out well. Negative social expectations also are part of general negative expectations in everyday life, or *pessimism*—viewing life with a negative and bleak outlook. This negative outlook can have different shadings. It may be infused with feelings of helplessness and despair; consist of problem-ridden ruminations and preoccupations with upsetting and disturbing events exaggerated out of proportion; involve anger, disgust, irritation, and frustration with others and life events; or represent a calmer variant of the latter with the individual feeling removed from, and unconcerned with, others and situations because these seem uninteresting, boring, or mundane.

The third criterion for judging pleasantness of temperament is the pleasant-unpleasant quality of conversation topics. Are the topics of your conversation generally about positive, exciting, happy, and satisfying experiences or are they typically about problems, difficulties, and dissatisfaction with people or situations, or about mishaps or accidents.

Self-examination in terms of these three criteria should help you decide whether you lean more toward a pleasant or an unpleasant temperament. Or, you may decide you are somewhere in the middle of these two extremes in that you possess a balance of both the pleasant and unpleasant qualities. Assuming you still are uncertain, Chapter 4 should be of help. If you decide you have a pleasant temperament, give yourself a pleasantness score of +1 for later use. Give yourself a score of -1 for an unpleasant temperament. Use a score of zero if you feel you are neutral with respect to pleasantness-unpleasantness.

Arousability

The second step in assessing temperament is to identify your level of arousability. Remember that we all react to sudden increases in environmental uncertainty (complexity, variation, speed of change, unpredictable quality, novelty) with a sharp rise in arousal followed by a gradual decline of arousal back to normal levels. Those of us who are arousable, however, have a larger than average increase in arousal and a slower than average decline back to normal. In contrast, unarousable persons show a smaller increase in arousal and a faster drop back to normal.

These differences arise because arousable persons process more of the information in their environments. Every situation has some important or central components and many less important or peripheral parts. For instance, if you are playing a game of tennis, the important elements are your opponent's actions, the trajectory of the ball, and your strategy of play. Less important components of this situation are your opponent's tennis outfit, presence of bystanders, noise from a construction crew working in the neighborhood, the fact that you had a quarrel with your mate before the game, or that the court reminds you of another one you played on in England.

An arousable person in this situation is liable to be influenced by more of the peripheral stimuli. He might feel self-conscious because others are observing the game, become distracted by the noise from the construction work, or be preoccupied with the quarrel he had a couple of hours before the game. In contrast, while playing, a less arousable person will tend not to notice or think about the irrelevant or less relevant parts of the situation. This example illustrates how arousable persons go through many everyday events, automatically and unconsciously, processing more of the irrelevant elements. It also shows how the unarousable are automatically and unconsciously selective, attending only to the more important aspects in various situations.

To decide whether you are arousable or unarousable, it is important that you decide how much attention and thought you devote to peripheral elements of your surroundings and activities. You might break this down into your reactions to stimuli in various sense modalities. Are you aware of, and sensitive to, low-volume hums, background noises, or music while doing conceptual work? Are you distracted or bothered by moderately loud music while working or eating? Are you particularly sensitive to extremes in temperature? Are you unusually responsive to textures of materials that come into contact with your skin? For instance, do you find it difficult to wear certain materials because the textures disturb and distract you? Again, are you especially sensitive to pleasant or unpleasant odors such as perfumes, the smell of various foods, the smell of garbage, or another's body odor?

In answering these questions for yourself, try to compare your reactions to those of others. In general, compared with others, are you more or less sensitive to, and aware of, these peripheral stimuli as you go through your daily activities? If you have less sensitivity to irrelevant stimuli, then you are unarousable; in contrast, greater awareness implies higher arousability.

Aside from general sensory sensitivity, you need to consider how easily you become emotional. How much are you affected by the joy or sorrow of others? Do strong emotions have a lasting effect on you? Do complicated situations and changing and unpredictable events affect you strongly in an emotional way? For instance, when you enter an unfamiliar situation where many things are happening at once, does it take you longer than most others to get used to it and to calm down? Do you startle easily? Does it take you long to overcome negative feelings from a quarrel, an insult, or a failure?

Also, remember the discussion of "external" information (one's surroundings, the people in them, and events) versus "internal" information (including memories and imagery relating to recent or long-past experiences). While in the same situation with the unarousable, the arousable generate more information internally and thus must process more complex (internal plus external) information.

You need to decide whether you are the kind of person who dwells on intense emotional episodes in your day-to-day life and on distant, but emotionally significant, past events. Do memories of such events frequently intrude into your daily activities and become part of your "psychological baggage"? Or, are you the kind of person who gets over emotional experiences easily, sets them aside, and proceeds on to other things with a reasonably unencumbered mind?

Consider all the various elements of arousability, and review Chapter 5 if needed, so you can give yourself an arousability score. You need to decide whether you have an arousable temperament (and give yourself an arousability score of +1 for later use), an unarousable temperament (score of -1), or one that is neutral or in between the two extremes of arousability (score of zero).

Dominance

The third step in assessing your temperament is to decide whether you are dominant or submissive. Do you typically control, take charge of, and influence people, events, and situations, or are you generally controlled, influenced, and guided by others and by situations or circumstances?

Remember that, in social situations, dominant persons tend to talk more than others and to become the center of attention. They talk louder and with less hesitation and, in some cases, smile and nod less often. The dominant are prone to interrupt the speech of others mid-stream. More importantly, they readily express and act upon their evaluations of people, events, and places— not hesitating to say what they like or dislike and prefer or want, or to act in accordance with their evaluations and desires.

In contrast, the submissive talk less and softer; their speech is likely to be slow and halting or even to involve errors and slips. They relinquish the center stage to others and, in some cases, smile and nod frequently to show agreement. Again, more importantly, submissive persons are reluctant to express their evaluations and desires or to act according to their likes and dislikes when such actions run counter to the opinions or wishes of others.

Examine you social style and general life style in terms of these characteristics of dominant and submissive individuals and review Chapter 6 if needed. You should be able to decide whether you have a dominant temperament (and give yourself a dominance score of +1 for later use), a submissive temperament (score of –1), or one that is neutral or in between these two extremes (score of zero).

Your Temperament Profile

Let us say this process of self-examination leads you to the conclusion that you have distinct (i.e., non-neutral) characteristics on each of the three dimensions of temperament. In that case, you can label the combination with one of the following eight names. The label you choose will identify the chapter which you might want to review from time to time (e.g., Chapter 10 for "relaxed").

Exuberant = +P +A +D = pleasant, arousable, dominant

Dependent = +P +A −D = pleasant, arousable, submissive

Relaxed   = +P −A +D = pleasant, unarousable, dominant

Docile   = +P −A −D = pleasant, unarousable, submissive

Hostile   = −P +A +D = unpleasant, arousable, dominant

Anxious   = −P +A −D = unpleasant, arousable, submissive

Disdainful = −P −A +D = unpleasant, unarousable, dominant

Bored   = −P −A −D = unpleasant, unarousable, submissive

More than likely, you will judge yourself to have distinct characteristics on one or two dimensions of temperament and decide you are neutral on the remaining dimension(s). If two characteristics are clearly defined, then your temperament is a cross between two of the eight basic types. For example, supposing a person decides he is pleasant and dominant, but is neutral on arousability. In that case, he has characteristics of both the relaxed and the exuberant.

The apparent confusion in this example is resolved easily by considering the situations in which he behaves. He is likely to behave like the relaxed when he is in unarousing situations or is dealing with low-uncertainty investments. In contrast, he probably will behave like the exuberant in arousing situations or while dealing with high-uncertainty investments.

When you read the following section, you will be assigning a score to the arousing quality of your life circumstances. For the individual in the preceding example, life circumstances may turn out to be arousing; in that case, he probably would behave like the exuberant. In contrast, if his life circumstances were unarousing, he would be likely to behave like the relaxed.

One final possibility is that you will decide you have a distinct characteristic on only one dimension of temperament and are neutral on the remaining two. In that case, your temperament is easy to define and understand. If, for example, you conclude you have a pleasant temperament but are neutral on arousability and on dominance, then pleasantness would be the most distinctive aspect of your temperament and you may want to review Chapter 4.

Save the numerical scores you have assigned yourself on each of the three temperament dimensions because you will need them in the following chapter to select the level of investment uncertainty that suits you.

SELF-ASSESSMENT OF LIFE CIRCUMSTANCES

Our life circumstances tend to change from time to time and, at all times, it is important to track the emotional effects these circumstances have on us. For most people, the major components of their life situations are their social and family lives and their work. The dimensions of pleasure-displeasure, arousal-nonarousal, and dominance-submissiveness can be used separately and applied to each of these components.

Pleasantness

Think of your family and social life and include recreational activities that you have alone or with family members. How do you assess its overall pleasantness? Examine the following descriptions and decide which group predominates.

Pleasant. Comfortable, relaxed, happy; easy, smooth, loving and gratifying relationships; interesting recreational activities; satisfactory finances.

Unpleasant. Boring; uncomfortable, tense, unhappy, or conflictive; lonely; unsatisfactory and even antagonistic relationships; absence of fun and recreational activities; financial difficulties.

You need to form a mental average of the pleasant elements and balance these off against the unpleasant ones. Give your family/social life a score of +1 on pleasantness if pleasant elements clearly outweigh unpleasant ones. Give it a score of +.5 if pleasant elements are moderately more predominant relative to unpleasant ones. Give it a score of zero if pleasant and unpleasant elements occur with about equal frequency and intensity. If, on the other hand, unpleasant element clearly outweigh pleasant ones, give your family/social life a pleasantness score of –1. Give it a score of –.5 if unpleasant elements are moderately more predominant compared with pleasant ones.

Next, apply the same evaluation process to your work situation. Decide which of the following two sets predominates.

Pleasant. Good pay; interesting work; work not stimulating, but pleasant and comfortable; comfortable and pleasant relationships with coworkers; opportunities to learn more and get ahead; a feeling that you are doing something useful and important.

Unpleasant. Inadequate pay; boring or uninteresting work; frequent problems; inconsiderate supervisors or management; awkward or conflictive relationships with coworkers; lack of opportunities for self-advancement, learning, and promotions; a feeling that you are doing work that does not have much significance or value in the broader scheme of things.

As with the ratings you assigned your family and social situation, use the balance between the pleasant and unpleasant elements above to assign your work pleasantness-unpleasantness scores ranging from +1 to –1.

Next, average the pleasantness scores you assigned your family/social situation and your work. This should provide a reasonable estimate of the pleasantness-unpleasantness of your life circumstances at this point in time. Supposing, for instance, you have a happy, satisfying, and trouble-free family situation to which you assigned a score of +1. Supposing also, that the pleasant elements at your job moderately outweigh the unpleasant ones, yielding a score of +.5. Then, overall, your life circumstances would receive a pleasantness score of +.75. On the other hand, if your family life is unsatisfying and involves frequent conflicts and numerous financial problems (–1) and your work life is boring, unrewarding, and seems to be going nowhere (–1), then the overall pleasantness rating of your life circumstances is –1.

Arousing Quality

You need to assign a score to your family/social life, including your recreational activities, and a separate score to your work. First, rate your family/social life by deciding which of the following groups of factors predominates.

Arousing. Frequent changes in daily routines; new and varied activities; a heavy social calendar involving friends and relatives; intense positive or negative relationships with family members; uncertainty about major upcoming events; drastic changes brought on by changes in residence, a move to another city, childbirth, assumption of a large mortgage, divorce, or death.

Unarousing. Fixed daily routines that are highly predictable; absence of new and varied social activities; contacts primarily with familiar friends and relatives; low level of involvement with family members; reasonable certainty as to what to expect in the near and not too distant future; absence of sudden and drastic changes.

You need to form a mental average of the arousing elements and balance these off against the unarousing ones. Give your family and social life an arousing value of +1 if arousing elements clearly outweigh unarousing ones. Give it an arousing value of +.5 if arousing elements are moderately more predominant relative to unarousing ones. Give it a score of zero if arousing and unarousing elements balance each other off. If, on the other hand, unarousing elements clearly outweigh arousing ones, give your family/social life an arousing value of –1. Give it a score of –.5 if unarousing elements are moderately more predominant compared with arousing ones.

Use a parallel scoring system for your work by deciding which of the following two groups of elements predominates.

Arousing. Frequent changes in daily routines; no fixed schedule; new, varied, and unfamiliar tasks; numerous interactions with coworkers over the course of the day; frequent contacts with persons outside your company or organization; intense positive or negative emotional involvement with one or more coworkers; uncertainty about important upcoming changes; highly complex work; work-related travel; drastic changes at work, including promotions, demotions, new responsibilities, loss of work, or a new job.

Unarousing. Fixed daily routines and a generally predictable schedule; work involving repetition and application of well-developed skills; few interactions with coworkers; infrequent contacts with persons outside your company or organization; lack of emotional involvements with coworkers; a clear and predictable work outlook such that you know what to expect in the future; simple work; no drastic or sudden changes.

Depending on whether the arousing or unarousing elements predominate, assign your work a score anywhere from +1 (for clearly arousing) to –1 (for clearly unarousing). Next, average this score for your work with the score you assigned your family and social life to get a score for overall arousal from your life circumstances.

Dominance

You are dominant when you are influential in, or in control of, a situation. In contrast, you are submissive when others, situations, or events control and influence what happens to you. For your family and social life, you need to decide which of the following two sets of elements predominates.

Dominant. You plan the calendar of social events; you decide on purchases of important and large items that will be used for years to come; you strongly influence the type of food consumed; you determine family recreational activities; you have private areas at home that essentially are off limits to others; you decide which friendships the family cultivates or neglects; you decide on the timing and places of vacations; you control the family purse strings.

Submissive. Others plan the calendar of social events; others decide on important and large purchases; others strongly influence the type of food consumed; others determine the joint recreational activities of the family; you do not have a private area at home that is free of intrusions; others decide which friendships are important and which are not; others decide on, and plan, vacations; others control family finances.

Balance these two groups of factors against one another. Assign your family/social situation a dominance score of +1 if you are primarily in control and assign it a score of –1 if others are basically in control. Use a score of +.5 if dominant elements are moderately more predominant than submissive ones. Conversely, use a score of –.5 if submissive elements are moderately more predominant. If the two groups of factors balance each other, assign a score of zero.

For work, the comparable groups of factors are as follows.

Dominant. You decide what you are to do; you decide your own work schedule; you get to choose the people with whom you need to interact; you plan the activities of others and determine what they are to do; you can be yourself, not have to make any pretenses, and speak your mind; you control how hard you have to work; you determine how far up and ahead you can get in terms of income and position.

Submissive. Others decide what you are to do; others decide your work schedule; you have no choice as to with whom you must interact; others plan your activities and determine your tasks; you have to act like someone other than you are so as to be accepted or to get ahead; others control how hard you must work; others determine your salary and your promotions.

Balance these two groups of factors against one another and assign your job a dominance score of +1 if the first group clearly predominates; assign a dominance score of –1 if the second group clearly prevails. Select intermediate values of +.5 (and –.5) if the first (second) group predominates moderately. Assign a dominance score of zero if the two groups of factors roughly balance each other off.

Now, average the dominance scores for your family/social life with the score for your work. This average score should provide a reasonable estimate of the dominance-submissiveness you feel due to your life circumstances.

THE PROFILE OF YOUR LIFE CIRCUMSTANCES

The numerical scores you assigned your life circumstances on each of the pleasure, arousal, and dominance dimensions can be used to select a summary label. Use the following eight combinations to label the primary emotional impact of your life circumstances.

Exuberant = +P +A +D = pleasant, aroused, dominant

Dependent = +P +A –D = pleasant, aroused, submissive

Relaxed   = +P –A +D = pleasant, unaroused, dominant

Docile   = +P –A –D = pleasant, unaroused, submissive

Hostile   = –P +A +D = unpleasant, aroused, dominant

Anxious   = –P +A –D = unpleasant, aroused, submissive

Disdainful = –P –A +D = unpleasant, unaroused, dominant

Bored   = –P –A –D = unpleasant, unaroused, submissive

Let us say you judged your life circumstances to be conducive to feelings of pleasure (score of +.75), low arousal (score of -.5), and dominance (+.25). In that case, the appropriate label is "relaxed." This means that the combination of all elements in your work and home life is relaxing for you. Alternatively, if your life situation makes you feel unpleasant, unaroused, and submissive, then it has a boring effect on you.

You already are aware of the effects each of these eight emotional states has on one's approach to investing. So, by analyzing and scoring the emotional impact of your life circumstances, you can understand how your life situation (as distinct from your temperament) influences the way you invest.

As in the case of temperament, your life circumstances may have a neutral influence on one emotion dimension (e.g., dominance), but have distinctive effects on the remaining two dimensions (e.g., induce pleasure and low arousal). In that case, the overall emotional impact is a combination of relaxed and docile feelings and the corresponding two chapters are most relevant. In case your life circumstances have a non-neutral impact on only one dimension (e.g., arousal), then Chapter 5 is most relevant and worth reviewing.

SELF-ASSESSMENT OF INVESTMENT STYLE

Investment style is a pattern of investment behaviors that recurs frequently despite changes in investments and investment circumstances. To identify one's investment style, it is useful to write out a summary page on each past investment that has gone through a complete cycle of purchase and sale (or short sale and subsequent purchase).

Each summary should contain a brief description of the following items.

1. The item purchased or sold short, the dollar amount involved, and date of the transaction.
2. Your knowledge and technical proficiency in the area in which you invested.
3. Manner of selecting the investment. For example, was it someone else's advice or an article in a newspaper that led you to make the choice?
4. Time and effort spent investigating the particular investment before committing money to it.
5. Your investment goal in terms of income and capital appreciation.
6. Your strategy to achieve that goal.
7. Date of sale or covering of short position.
8. Circumstances that led you to complete the investment cycle. Was it another person's advice, your own decision based on your strategy that had been in place all along, a forced sale due to losses or to meet debt payments (margin calls), a sale due to a change in plans,

or an urgent need of the invested funds for living expenses?

9.   Percentage annualized return on the investment.

The following exemplifies a sample summary page.

Purchased 1,000 shares of stock Z on August 13, 1985, for $50,000. Had no expertise in the stock market at the time of purchase. Bought the stock on advice of a friend who invests in the stock market regularly and who recommended the purchase. I did not investigate the company specifically but took my friend's word it was a good one. My primary investment objective was capital appreciation because I was told the stock would move up sharply. My strategy was to hold the stock until my friend told me it was time to sell. I sold the stock on February 15, 1986, for $45,000 because even though the price first moved up a bit and I held on for additional profits, it next began a gradual decline and I could not afford a greater loss. Also, my friend told me he no longer was certain about the prospects of the stock, and a stock broker I called told me he was neutral on it. Having held it for approximately six months, my annualized return was:

$$[(\$45,000 - \$50,000)/\$50,000] \times (12/6) \times 100 = -20\%.$$

Here is another sample.

My parents own an art gallery so I am intimately familiar with prices and trends in art. Two years ago, I had an opportunity to purchase a painting from a moderately well-known artist who was having some financial difficulties. I paid $3,200 for the painting. My investment goal was capital appreciation and my strategy was to hold on until he had a successful exhibition which would create demand for his work. He recently had a very successful one-man exhibit, and I was able to sell the painting through my parents' contacts for $12,000. Having held it for approximately 24 months, my annualized return was:

$$[(\$12,000 - \$3200)/\$3200] \times (12/24) \times 100 = 137.5\%$$

A few of these single-page summaries typically will reveal certain recurrent patterns. The particulars of each investment, as summarized, can vary considerably. For example, one can always think of an excuse, any excuse, to justify a premature sale. Or, the circumstances under which one makes a hasty purchase might seem different from one investment to another. *While superficial characteristics differ when comparing various investments, the basic patterns remain intact. The key idea, then, is to abstract an investment pattern (or patterns) from many particular, superficially dissimilar, and seemingly unrelated actions in different investments.*

Chapter 12 contains sample patterns abstracted from transaction summaries of one stock market investor (Table 12–1). It would be useful to review that table at this point. Each of the patterns in that table was translated into a trading rule. The rules were designed by that investor to avoid losses due to harmful patterns.

In reading the many examples throughout this volume, you undoubtedly have come across trading patterns that are descriptive of your own investment style. The sample patterns in Table 17–1 should help you identify some of your investment patterns. The table describes problem patterns, since one tends to overlook these more easily.

Table 17–1 contains only some of the patterns mentioned in previous chapters. Use this list along with your summaries to make up your own list of patterns. As in the case of the sample patterns given in Chapter 12, summarize your own patterns with brief, single-sentence, descriptions.

᠊ᴜᴏɪᴇ 17–1 Undesirable Investment Patterns

- Investing in areas where one has minimal expertise.

- Investing in specific instruments or properties that one fails to investigate carefully due to overconfidence in one's knowledge of the investment field.

- Making impulsive and careless purchases and sales.

- Forced sales due to overconfidence and excessive "leverage" (large percentage of purchase price paid with borrowed funds).

- Forced sales necessitated because more capital was committed than one could afford. Urgent financial needs elsewhere dictated the sale.

- Investing after very careful study and buying at advantageous prices, but selling impulsively and carelessly because one is angry or upset with the slow progress of the investment.

- Investing carelessly and being immediately confronted with a loss. Avoiding admission of the serious error by convincing oneself that the investment is a sound long-term holding.

- Holding an investment through a lengthy period of paper losses and selling at the first opportunity to break even.

- Making purchases and sales on the basis of recommendations of others or recommendations found in financial magazines or newspapers.

- Following the crowd in speculative markets.

- Treating investments as a sport or play. Making careless purchases and sales simply to generate excitement and/or relief from boredom or depression—the gambler's style.

Table 17–1 (Continued)

• Holding on to investments that generate losses just to prove someone else was wrong and gave bad advice.

• Being timid and failing to take advantage of extremely timely and beneficial investments even when one has the necessary financial resources.

• Being knowledgeable, but impatient. Knowing the correct and opportune times to buy or sell but not having enough patience to wait for those times. Buying prematurely and at higher prices or selling too soon and with lower profits than otherwise possible.

• Easily getting caught up in the excitement of markets that heat up temporarily. Inadvertently becoming more active and making unnecessary trades because of the emotional contagion of fast-paced markets.

• Inability to follow an investment plan or strategy. Being discouraged easily by losses and giving up by selling.

• Being impatient and buying too soon in declining markets.

• Selling prematurely to get into something else that seems more promising or to experiment with another strategy for which one has higher expectations.

• Selling at a loss due to lack of confidence and knowledge.

• Failure to follow a strategy because of lack of confidence or knowledge.

Table 17–1 (Continued)

- Having exaggerated high expectations before purchase and becoming disappointed soon after purchase because the investment does not meet those expectations.

- Selling prematurely due to anger at the investment, the investment broker, or oneself. Selling because anger generated in other areas of one's life reduces one's tolerance for frustration.

- Being inflexible. Unable to use sound advice and information to alter a flawed strategy or to get out of a loss-prone investment. Stubborn clinging to bad investments that result in intolerably large losses.

- Using one's investments as conversation topics and tending to brag about occasional successes.

- Posing as an expert and giving investment advice to acquaintances and even strangers.

Forced self-examination along these lines helps you become aware and conscious of emotional factors in your investing. Make it a point to review these written abstracts of your investment style *before* you make any investment purchase or sale. Once you know your patterns, you readily will detect whether a certain inclination to buy or sell is reminiscent of an established pattern. The recognition will serve as a warning signal to stop and think. If you become aware that a trading decision is motivated emotionally, you can avoid the trade temporarily and search for sound and realistic reasons for action. If there are none, you can hold off on the trade altogether and wait for a more opportune time.

In sum, by abstracting your investment patterns, you can identify the emotional sources of your investment problems and make them conscious and explicit. Review these patterns periodically and revise them if needed. Read your list carefully prior to any investment transaction. This should help you reduce the effects of emotional forces and increase the contribution of rational considerations in your investing.

Chapter 18

Selecting a Suitable Level of Investment Uncertainty

THE ROLE OF TEMPERAMENT

A general guideline is needed to summarize all earlier considerations of suitable investment uncertainty for any individual. The following equation does just that, using P for pleasantness, A for arousability, and D for dominance.

Suitable investment uncertainty = +P −2A +D(1−.5A)

To use the equation, we substitute +1 and −1 for high and low values, respectively, on each of the pleasure, arousability, and dominance dimensions.

Coefficients in the equation show the direction and strength of each effect. It is seen that arousability has a very strong (detrimental) effect on investing, that pleasantness has a strong (beneficial) effect, and that strength of the (beneficial) effect of dominance depends on arousability. When arousability is low (or −1), the term D(1−.5A) becomes +1.5D, showing a strong beneficial effect of dominance. For high arousability (+1), the same term becomes .5D, showing a weak beneficial effect of dominance. Thus, when one is unarousable, being dominant is highly beneficial and one can invest in high-uncertainty areas. In comparison, when one is arousable, being dominant has a much weaker beneficial effect on investing.

For a hostile person who has an unpleasant (–1), arousable (+1), and dominant (+1) temperament, the equation yields,

$$-1 -2 \times 1 +1(1-.5 \times 1) = -2.5$$

The resulting number, –2.5, is significant only in comparison with suitable uncertainty levels calculated for other temperament types. Table 18–1 contains results of these computations for all eight temperament categories. Separately, uncertainty values are ranked from highest (rank = 1) to lowest (rank = 8).

Table 18–1 Suitable Investment Uncertainty Levels

Temperament	Components	Suitable Uncertainty Value	Investment Uncertainty Rank
Exuberant	+P +A +D	–0.5	4.5
Dependent	+P +A –D	–1.5	6
Relaxed	+P –A +D	4.5	1
Docile	+P –A –D	1.5	3
Hostile	–P +A +D	–2.5	7
Anxious	–P +A –D	–3.5	8
Disdainful	–P –A +D	2.5	2
Bored	–P –A –D	–0.5	4.5

Note. +P and –P stand for pleasant and unpleasant temperament, respectively. +A and –A represent arousable and unarousable, and +D and –D represent dominant and submissive, temperament, respectively. Higher "suitable uncertainty values" mean an individual can take on more uncertain investments. In the last column, these values are ranked from highest (1) to lowest (8). The Bored and Exuberant are tied with a ranking of 4.5.

Pleasantness-unpleasantness of temperament actually is a continuum with many gradations ranging from extreme pleasantness on to extreme unpleasantness. The same applies to arousability and dominance.

So far, for convenience of discussion, we simply have divided each of these three dimensions into upper versus lower halves. Sometimes, a better way to classify people on these dimensions is to segment each dimension into three ranges: two opposing extremes and the neutral middle, with one-third of the population in each range. When this three-way classification is used, the label "arousable," for instance, refers to the third of the population composing the upper range of the arousable-unarousable continuum, "unarousable" applies to the third composing the lower range, with the remaining third of the population constituting the neutral, middle range on arousability.

A person, then, can place within the upper, middle, or lower range of pleasantness-unpleasantness; that same person can place within any one of three segments of arousability, and, separately, within any one of three segments of dominance-submissiveness.

Our general equation can be used to calculate suitable investment uncertainty values when each dimension is divided into thirds. In that case, +1, 0, and −1 are substituted for high, neutral, and low values, respectively, on each of the three dimensions. Thus, for someone who is neutral on pleasantness (0) but who is arousable (+1) and submissive (−1), the equation yields,

$$0 - 2 \times 1 - 1(1 - .5 \times 1) = -2.5$$

showing a rather low suitable level of investment uncertainty. This person is a cross between the dependent and the anxious and the score −2.5 turns out to be the average of scores for dependent and anxious persons given in Table 18–1.

Someone who is pleasant (+1), neutral on arousability (0), and neutral on dominance (0) gets a score of +1. Another person who is neutral on all three dimensions gets a score of zero.

Non-neutral or more extreme temperament qualities, thus, are more distinctive and highlight a person's chances of success versus failure in investing. Let us say, Elizabeth is neutral on pleasantness and on dominance and places in the upper third on arousability. For her, our general discussion of arousable persons in Chapter 5 and their approaches to, and problems with, investments is most relevant.

The effect of Elizabeth's temperament on her investments is easy to understand since she is extreme on only one of three basic temperament characteristics, arousability. The equation yields a score of –2 for Elizabeth, showing that she should restrict herself to low-uncertainty investments.

Consider David who is neutral on pleasantness (0), in the lower third on arousability (–1), and the upper third on dominance (+1). His unarousable and dominant characteristics have the most bearing on his investment style. For him, our discussions of unarousable persons in Chapter 5, and of dominant ones in Chapter 6, are most relevant.

Alternatively, David can be viewed as a cross between the relaxed and the disdainful. So, to understand his investing, it is useful also to refer to our discussions of these two temperament types. For David, the equation yields,

$$0 - 2 \times (-1) + 1[1 - .5(-1)] = 3.5.$$

This shows David can handle very high-uncertainty investments. The result is expected since he is a cross between the relaxed (score of 4.5 in Table 18–1) and the disdainful (score of 2.5), with both being highly competent to deal with high-uncertainty investments.

For another case, consider Maria who is unpleasant (–1) and arousable (+1) but neutral on dominance (0). She represents a cross between the hostile and the anxious and can be described in terms of a combination of those two patterns. In her case, the equation yields,

$$-1 -2 \times 1 +0(1-.5 \times 1) = -3$$

which is a very low score. This score is expected for Maria because of the averaged effects for the hostile (score of –2.5 in Table 18–1) and the anxious (score of –3.5).

THE ROLE OF LIFE CIRCUMSTANCES

In addition to temperament, life circumstances also generate recurrent and distinctive emotional states. Our equation for suitable investment uncertainty is applicable as well to life circumstances. For the latter, in the equation, P stands for pleasure-displeasure, A for arousal-nonarousal, and D for dominance-submissiveness from life circumstances.

For example, John is arousable but neutral on pleasantness and on dominance. His life circumstances (mainly his work and his home life) are pleasant and make him feel dominant. The combined result of his temperament and life circumstances, then, is that he feels exuberant. Thus, his investment actions are likely to resemble those of the exuberant.

A more exact way to calculate suitable investment uncertainty for John is to compute that value for his temperament and separately for his life circumstances and then to average the two figures. The value for his temperament (P=0, A=+1, D=0) is –2. The corresponding value for his life circumstances (P=+1, A=0, D=+1) is +2. The average of these two figures is zero which approximates the –0.5 figure given in Table 18–1 for exuberant persons.

In general, then, to estimate the uncertainty level that an individual should seek in investing, we simply average the suitable investment uncertainty value for his temperament with the suitable investment uncertainty value for his life circumstances.

STRESS

One useful application is in assessing the effects of stress. Stressful life circumstances are unpleasant, arousing, and make one feel submissive (P=–1, A=+1, D=–1). Using these values, our equation yields,

$$-1 - 2 \times 1 - 1[1 - .5 \times 1] = -3.5$$

which, incidentally, is the figure given in Table 18–1 for those with anxious temperaments.

Our life circumstances can become stressful temporarily during various periods. Since we average the effect of life circumstances with the effect of temperament, it is seen that stress lowers any person's ability to deal with high-uncertainty investments. Even someone with a relaxed temperament would need to aim for an uncertainty level of 0.5 (the average of –3.5 for stress and 4.5 for temperament) under stressful conditions.

The implication is that we all need to lower the uncertainty levels of our investments to compensate for temporary increases in stress at work or at home. A relaxed person who, for instance, trades actively in commodities or stocks would be advised to drastically curtail the frequency of her trades or even to employ a managed fund during periods of high stress. Once stress is diminished, she can resume her habitual trading pattern.

CHANGES IN LIFE SITUATIONS

As we have seen, life circumstances influence pleasure, arousal, and dominance levels independently and in a great variety of ways. Consider a factory foreman who is assigned additional important responsibilities together with higher pay. This means a probable increase in pleasure and arousal with dominance remaining at its existing high level, so, P=+1, A=+1, and D=+1. Our equation yields a value of –0.5 for his life circumstances which is the same figure as that for exuberant persons.

When equally dominant partners in a marriage begin to have conflicts, displeasure and arousal increase while dominance stays neutral. In this case, with P=–1, A=+1, and D=0, our equation yields a value of –3 for suitable investment uncertainty.

It follows that to assess the impact of changing life situations, we do not rely exclusively on the concept of stress. Instead, we consider the independent and specific ways in which pleasure, arousal, and dominance are affected. A suitable investment uncertainty value is calculated readily for any combination of pleasure, arousal, and dominance and shows how investment choices can be made to adjust to changing life circumstances.

Awareness of the emotional impact of life circumstances is critical to help recognize unconscious reasons for an impulsive and sudden need to change one's investment strategy. Frieda, for instance, uses methodical and slow-moving tactics to invest in stocks and has had moderate and consistent success over a long period of time. But, at some point, she may lose patience with the slow pace of her investments and feel a strong urge to experiment with very high-uncertainty financial futures. Being aware of how life circumstances influence emotions, Frieda would be able to examine recent developments in her work or social life and determine whether onset of boredom, for instance, led to the irrational urge to change investment tactics.

Generally, anytime investors feel an unexplained urge to change investment tactics or to explore new and unfamiliar investments, they would be well advised initially to refrain from any action and instead to consider recent changes in their social lives and work.

The preceding examples illustrate how investors can easily recognize and quantify the emotional effects of changing life situations. They, therefore, could determine whether the urge to change investments or investment tactics was rational and beneficial or whether it was emotional, reflex-like, and potentially harmful.

Assume that Gwen suddenly is confronted with a variety of job-related problems and feels an unexplained need to stop investing actively, even though her investments are profitable. Instead, she may want to place all her funds in a savings account. In this case, the desired change is beneficial. Job-related problems increase stress and a temporary decrease in investment uncertainty would provide a welcome balance.

In comparison, consider Howard who suddenly is confronted with intense job-related problems and wants to increase his trading pace or experiment with unfamiliar and fast-paced investments. Examining this urge in terms of our framework would alert Howard to its dangers. He might recognize that his hostile temperament, in combination with increased stress from work, is increasing his impatience and driving him to more desperate efforts at investing.

Our emotion-based framework is unique in that it allows us to analyze the distinct effects of situations and people using similar concepts. We use the concept of temperament (or emotional characteristics) to describe people and employ the analogous concept of recurrent emotional states to describe the impact of life circumstances. We thus can compare and average diverse influences of temperament and life situations on investments. Our equation, and the accompanying table, summarize how one can select investment uncertainty to fit a particular temperament, a set of life circumstance, or any combination of these.

Chapter 19

Epilogue

The suggestion that our relationships to our investments resemble some of our most intimate relationships was not made lightly at the beginning of this volume. Few human activities bring forth the breadth and intensity of emotions aroused by investments. And, it is such stimulation at the most basic, uncensored, and primitive levels of experience, that reveals us the most.

The foundation of character or personality is temperament, or emotional makeup. Consistent patterns of behavior associated with temperament define the individual—the distinctive psychological entity that is a person. Temperament often is hidden from view because of the process of socialization and learned control over one's self presentation. However, when people are tickled at their emotional cores, temperament is exposed readily.

Under extreme emotional circumstances, choices are greatly narrowed and deliberate control over behavioral options is reduced. We tend to bypass socially "proper" behaviors we may have learned in the course of socialization and fall back on stereotypic, atavistic actions which for each person have an almost reflex-like quality.

Investing entails some of these extreme situations and, thereby, exposes the uncensored patterns of action. This is how, even with limited exposure to investments, people tend to rapidly settle down into a consistent style of dealing with their investments. Even casual observation of investors leads one to recognize the timid, the overconfident, the greedy, the one who can delay gratification, the braggart or exhibitionist, the methodical, the cautious, the conformist, the trend setter, or the playful.

Our framework exposes the close association between investment style and temperament. It provides the conceptual tools needed to categorize all possible temperament types and their correlated investment styles. In addition, it supplies explanations of the emotional effects of life circumstances and involvement with different types of investments.

Specific investment actions are influenced by temperament, emotional impact of life circumstances, and uncertainty level of investments. Since there is not much we can do to modify temperament and often we cannot readily alter our life circumstances, the important area on which to concentrate is the choice of investment uncertainty. To do this properly, we need to understand the level of uncertainty to which we are drawn instinctively and whether this level is appropriate for our temperament and our life circumstances.

Readers now are in a position to determine whether the investments they make are too high, or too low, in uncertainty and, if so, set out deliberately to chart alternative courses to investing that are suited more to their emotional (temperament and life circumstance) needs. Having done so, they also will be better equipped to monitor their own investments and to recognize ever-present temptations to seek apparent shortcuts or easier solutions and to deviate from, or abandon, long-term investment plans.

For all of us, adherence to long-range plans is easier when hasty investment actions are avoided. Hasty decisions and actions are usually prompted by heightened arousal; that is, excessive and undesirable emotionality. Instead, to control emotional inclinations in investing, purchases and sales should be considered at leisure and during preselected periods of the day or week when one can think out carefully the effects of one's temperament and life circumstances on the timing and choice of transactions.

Most investment difficulties arise when individuals intuitively select, or are inadvertently led to, higher-uncertainty investments than they can deal with from an emotional standpoint. Dependent and anxious persons, who generally are timid and avoid high-uncertainty investments, are nevertheless occasionally drawn into such situations by conforming to the crowd—following a popular consensus that certain investments are easy and highly profitable.

In the absence of strong crowd conviction, anxious and dependent persons err in the direction of selecting extreme low-uncertainty (very safe, low return) investments. Also, once they have been hurt because of participation in speculative markets, their timidity increases, leading them to adhere to the safest investments for many years at end. Thus, the anxious or dependent typically aim too low in terms of desired returns and occasionally err by aiming far too high.

Bored and exuberant individuals frequently are attracted to higher-uncertainty investments than they can cope with because, for them, investments are sources of fun and excitement. For the exuberant, risky, fast-paced investments provide yet another avenue of playful activity and adventure. For the bored, on the other hand, hope, excitement, and the highly active pace of these investments provide escape from an intolerable emotional condition.

But, investing is not a form of play, nor is it a constructive way to compensate for boredom or despair. Those who, like the exuberant or the bored, approach investments with a gambler's attitude seeking thrills, are doomed to failure. *A far more constructive attitude is to expect to be bored while investing!* Successful investing is work requiring careful study and preparation. It often is serious, difficult, and tiresome, and requires one to be deliberate, methodical, and to keep emotional reactions at bay.

Hostile persons also are attracted to more uncertainty than they can deal with successfully because of their over-confidence and tendency to regard investments as an arena of combat. They are drawn to investments where confrontation with other investors is most salient—someone else loses when you gain, and vice versa.

Then, there are those who do not do as well as they might because, being timid, they restrict themselves unduly to low-uncertainty investments. Docile persons, who actually can succeed at moderate-uncertainty investments, often fail to make use of this temperament-related advantage.

It also is important to remember that for all, particularly the arousable, high-uncertainty investments can be a severe drain on energies and psychological well-being. In several case histories described, involvement in high-uncertainty investments led to severe strains in investors' abilities to conduct their everyday affairs, including their abilities to work effectively, thus jeopardizing their single most important source of steady income.

Those who continue to struggle with investments which are inappropriately high in uncertainty relative to their temperaments or life circumstances not only fail to produce meaningful incomes from those investments but damage their chances of improved performance at their regular jobs. In addition, they increase the strains in their personal and family lives, sometimes resulting in drug addictions, divorce, loss of regular work, or a variety of psychosomatic ailments.

In short, investment difficulties or unsatisfactory investment performance result when we either aim too high (take on too much uncertainty) or aim too low. Our program of self-assessment can help investors gain detailed and accurate knowledge of their individual temperaments, investments styles, and life circumstances, and then translate these assessments into lists of investment guidelines.

Pinpointing strengths and limitations due to temperament is foremost in a program of self-assessment. Readers are well advised to annotate those sections of this volume which are most appropriate for understanding their own temperaments and ways in which their automatic emotional reactions result in beneficial or harmful investment actions. Once one is aware of the latter, it is easier to select investments which make the best uses of the strengths and where temperament-related limitations are less important. For example, persons who are impatient purposefully could select an investment medium which minimizes dangers due to impatience. They would, thus, avoid commodities or the stock market which are highly liquid and where purchases and sales are made with great ease. They instead could invest in less liquid vehicles such as real estate where even the impatient are forced to wait for extended periods in-between trades.

I am reminded of one particular acquaintance who sold a highly profitable family business for several million dollars and decided to retire. However, being used to an active work life, he was unable to enjoy the slow pace of retirement and was drawn to the stock market. Over the course of three years, and because of hasty and impulsive trading techniques, he lost over ninety percent of his capital. At that point, economic considerations forced him to withdraw from the market and to go to work as a real estate agent. Being an enterpreneur at heart, he used his income from real estate work to purchase small homes to generate rental income. He continued to accumulate real estate at a slow pace and held on to most of his acquisitions. Over the course of just a few years, he amassed considerable real estate holdings and wealth. His spectacular success in real estate was in sharp contrast to his dismal failure in the stock market. The forced slower pace of transactions in real estate investments probably played a major role in the difference.

In the preceding example, initial involvement in real estate was determined mostly by external, chance factors, including the need to make a living in the absence of technical or professional training. Daily exposure to real estate transactions led to an interest to invest in that area, and success resulted from the fortuitous selection of an area of investment that minimized the effects of a major temperament-related handicap.

When they occur, the successful matches between temperament and investment choices often are made intuitively and without conscious thought. Typically, the effects of temperament and emotions on investment choices and actions cannot be put into words and remain unverbalized or unconscious. The major thrust of this volume was to make explicit and conscious the emotional substrate which determines investment-related actions.

Specifically, our analyses were designed to expose and describe the regular patterns whereby strong emotional reactions to investing trigger automatic and reflex-like investment behaviors. Once the patterns are made explicit and are recognized by investors, there is a marked improvement in ability to influence and regulate investment actions compared with when the latter have an intuitive and unconscious base.

Awareness, and explicit formulation, of one's own handicaps leads to a better organized plan of action to compensate for those weaknesses than when there is little awareness, or rational analysis, of the source of problems. Most people are subjected to difficulties and losses with their investments at some time or another. Better understanding of the ways in which their temperaments and life circumstances contribute to these difficulties can be of considerable value in deliberately selecting, and adhering to, alternative strategies.

Increased awareness does not guarantee investment success. Nevertheless, it goes a long way toward selecting appropriate investments and strategies of investing and toward consistent adherence to plans that are made carefully and under calm circumstances.

References

1. Mehrabian, A. (1976). *Manual for the question-naire measure of stimulus screening and arousability.* (Available from Albert Mehrabian, P. O. Box 2568, Monterey, CA 93942.)

2. Mehrabian, A. (1977). A questionnaire measure of individual differences in stimulus screening and associated differences in arousability. *Environmental Psychology and Nonverbal Behavior, 1,* 89–103.

3. Mehrabian, A. (1978). Measures of individual differences in temperament. *Educational and Psychological Measurement, 38,* 1105–1117.

4. Mehrabian, A. (1981). *Silent messages: Implicit communication of emotions and attitudes* (2nd ed.). Belmont, CA: Wadsworth.

5. Mehrabian, A. (1987). *Eating characteristics and temperament: General measures and interrelationships.* New York, NY: Springer Verlag.

6. Mehrabian, A., & Hines, M. (1978). A questionnaire measure of individual differences in dominance-submissiveness. *Educational and Psychological Measurement, 38,* 479–484.

7. Mehrabian, A., & O'Reilly, E. (1980). Analysis of personality measures in terms of basic di-

mensions of temperament. *Journal of Personality and Social Psychology, 38,* 492–503.

8. Mehrabian, A., & Russell, J. A. (1974). The basic emotional impact of environments. *Perceptual and Motor Skills, 38,* 283–301.

9. Mehrabian, A., & Russell, J. A. (1974). A verbal measure of information rate for studies in environmental psychology. *Environment and Behavior,* 6, 233–252.

10. Russell, J. A., & Mehrabian, A. (1977). Evidence for a three-factor theory of emotions. *Journal of Research in Personality, 11,* 273–294.

Guide to References

Reference 9 supplies the theoretical and experimental basis for our concept of "uncertainty." The concept of "information rate," in that reference is equivalent to "uncertainty" as applied here to describe differences among investments.

The development of the measure for pleasantness-unpleasantness of temperament is given in Reference 3, that for arousability is given in References 1 and 2, and Reference 6 contains the description of the measure for dominance-submissiveness. Reference 7 shows how combinations of pleasantness-unpleasantness, high-low arousability, and dominance-submissiveness provide a comprehensive description of personality. Readers who wish to find all this material on temperament in one place are referred to Reference 5, Part I.

References 8 and 10 provide experimental evidence showing that pleasure-displeasure, arousal-nonarousal, and dominance-submissiveness are both necessary and sufficient for the comprehensive description and measurement of all emotion states.

Finally, Reference 4 contains extensive reviews of experimental findings in nonverbal communication and related subtle communication forms. I have relied on

these findings in suggesting the significance of mannerisms, movements, voice, and speech patterns in various
sections of the present volume.

Index

247